# The
# Wiersbe
## BIBLE STUDY SERIES

# The **Wiersbe**
## BIBLE STUDY SERIES

Learning

the Secret

of Living

by Faith

GENESIS 12–25

transforming lives together

THE WIERSBE BIBLE STUDY SERIES: GENESIS 12—25
Published by David C Cook
4050 Lee Vance View
Colorado Springs, CO 80918 U.S.A.

David C Cook Distribution Canada
55 Woodslee Avenue, Paris, Ontario, Canada N3L 3E5

David C Cook U.K., Kingsway Communications
Eastbourne, East Sussex BN23 6NT, England

The graphic circle C logo is a registered trademark of David C Cook.

All Scripture quotations in this study are taken from the Holy Bible, New
International Version®, NIV®. Copyright © 1973, 1984 by Biblica, Inc.™ Used
by permission of Zondervan. All rights reserved worldwide. www.zondervan.
com. The author has added italics to Scripture quotations for emphasis.

In the *Be Obedient* excerpts, unless otherwise noted, all Scripture quotations are taken
from the King James Version of the Bible. (Public Domain.) Scripture quotations marked
NKJV are taken from are taken from the New King James Version®. Copyright © 1982 by
Thomas Nelson, Inc. Used by permission. All rights reserved; NASB are taken from the New
American Standard Bible®, Copyright © 1960, 1995 by The Lockman Foundation. Used
by permission. (www.Lockman.org); ASV are taken from the American Standard Version.
(Public Domain); and NIV are taken from the Holy Bible, New International Version®, NIV®.

All excerpts taken from *Be Obedient*, second edition, published by David C Cook
in 2010 © 1991 Warren W. Wiersbe, ISBN 978-1-4347-6632-8.

ISBN 978-0-7814-0635-2
eISBN 978-0-7814-0858-5

The Team: Steve Parolini, Karen Lee-Thorp, Amy Konyndyk,
Nick Lee, Jack Campbell, Karen Athen
Series Cover Design: John Hamilton Design
Cover Photo: Veer

Printed in the United States of America
First Edition 2012

1 2 3 4 5 6 7 8 9 10

042512

# Contents

# Introduction to Genesis 12—25

## Living by Promises

In a world filled with insecurity and uncertainty, we must learn to walk by faith, or our lives will fall apart. This applies to *all* of God's children, regardless of how old we are or how long we have walked with the Lord.

Living by faith means obeying God's Word in spite of feelings, circumstances, or consequences. It means holding on to God's truth no matter how heavy the burden or how dark the day, knowing that He is working out His perfect plan.

*It means living by promises and not by expectations.*

## Abraham and Sarah

Abraham and Sarah are excellent teachers in the "school of faith," and we learn from them when we study Genesis 12—25. But faith is not something we study; it's something we practice. "By faith Abraham ... *obeyed*" (Heb. 11:8). If you want your faith to grow, be obedient!

As you study Genesis 12—25, your faith may be tested; but don't be afraid. Remember the words of Job: "But [God] knows the way that I take; when he has tested me, I will come forth as gold" (Job 23:10).

—*Warren W. Wiersbe*

# How to Use This Study

This study is designed for both individual and small-group use. We've divided it into eight lessons—each references one or more chapters in Warren W. Wiersbe's commentary *Be Obedient* (second edition, David C Cook, 2010). While reading *Be Obedient* is not a prerequisite for going through this study, the additional insights and background Wiersbe offers can greatly enhance your study experience.

The **Getting Started** questions at the beginning of each lesson offer you an opportunity to record your first thoughts and reactions to the study text. This is an important step in the study process as those "first impressions" often include clues about what it is your heart is longing to discover.

The bulk of the study is found in the **Going Deeper** questions. These dive into the Bible text and, along with helpful excerpts from Wiersbe's commentary, help you examine not only the original context and meaning of the verses but also modern application.

**Looking Inward** narrows the focus down to your personal story. These intimate questions can be a bit uncomfortable at times, but don't shy away from honesty here. This is where you are asked to stand before the mirror of God's Word and look closely at what you see. It's the place to take a good look at yourself in light of the lesson and search for ways in which you can grow in faith.

**Going Forward** is the place where you can commit to paper those things you want or need to do in order to better live out the discoveries you made in the Looking Inward section. Don't skip or skim through this. Take the time to really consider what practical steps you might take to move closer to Christ. Then share your thoughts with a trusted friend who can act as an encourager and accountability partner.

Finally, there is a brief **Seeking Help** section to close the lesson. This is a reminder for you to invite God into your spiritual-growth process. If you choose to write out a prayer in this section, come back to it as you work through the lesson and continue to seek the Holy Spirit's guidance as you discover God's will for your life.

## Tips for Small Groups

A small group is a dynamic thing. One week it might seem like a group of close-knit friends. The next it might seem more like a group of uncomfortable strangers. A small-group leader's role is to read these subtle changes and adjust the tone of the discussion accordingly.

Small groups need to be safe places for people to talk openly. It is through shared wrestling with difficult life issues that some of the greatest personal growth is discovered. But in order for the group to feel safe, participants need to know it's okay *not* to share sometimes. Always invite honest disclosure, but never force someone to speak if he or she isn't comfortable doing so. (A savvy leader will follow up later with a group member who isn't comfortable sharing in a group setting to see if a one-on-one discussion is more appropriate.)

Have volunteers take turns reading excerpts from Scripture or from the commentary. The more each person is involved even in the mundane tasks, the more they'll feel comfortable opening up in more meaningful ways.

The leader should watch the clock and keep the discussion moving. Sometimes there may be more Going Deeper questions than your group can cover in your available time. If you've had a fruitful discussion, it's okay to move on without finishing everything. And if you think the group is getting bogged down on a question or has taken off on a tangent, you can simply say, "Let's go on to question 5." Be sure to save at least ten to fifteen minutes for the Going Forward questions.

Finally, soak your group meetings in prayer—before you begin, during as needed, and always at the end of your time together.

# New Beginning

## (GENESIS 11:27—13:18)

*Before you begin …*

- *Pray for the Holy Spirit to reveal truth and wisdom as you go through this lesson.*
- *Read Genesis 11:27—13:18. This lesson references chapters 1 and 2 in* Be Obedient. *It will be helpful for you to have your Bible and a copy of the commentary available as you work through this lesson.*

## Getting Started

### From the Commentary

Salvation comes because God calls in grace and sinners respond by faith (Eph. 2:8–9; 2 Thess. 2:13–14). God called Abraham out of idolatry (Josh. 24:2) when he was in Ur of the Chaldees (Gen. 11:28, 31; 15:7; Neh. 9:7), a city devoted to Nannar, the moon-god. Abraham did not know the true God and had done nothing to deserve knowing Him, but God graciously called him. "Ye have not chosen me, but I have chosen you" (John 15:16).

Abraham was seventy-five years old when God called him, so age doesn't need to be an obstacle to faith. He trusted God for one hundred years (Gen. 25:7), and from his experience, we today can learn how to walk by faith and live to please the Lord.

Abraham was married to Sarah, his half sister (20:12), and they were childless. Yet God used them to found a great nation! "I called him [Abraham] alone, and blessed him, and increased him" (Isa. 51:2). Why would God call such an unlikely couple for such an important task? Paul gives you the answer in 1 Corinthians 1:26–31.

—*Be Obedient*, page 20

1. In what ways was the call of Abraham a new beginning? What made Abraham an unlikely candidate to be the focus of a radical new work of God? What does God's choice of Abraham tell you about God?

*More to Consider: We are not told how God appeared to Abraham, but in Genesis 12:1–3 we see that when He spoke to Abraham, it brought about the miracle of faith. "Faith comes from hearing the message, and the message is heard through the word of Christ" (Rom. 10:17). It was a call to separate Abraham from the corruption around him. Read 2 Corinthians 6:14—7:1. What do these verses teach us about true faith and the role faith played in Abraham's story?*

2. Choose one verse or phrase from Genesis 11:27—13:18 that stands out to you. This could be something you're intrigued by, something that makes you uncomfortable, something that puzzles you, something that resonates with you, or just something you want to examine further. Write that here.

## Going Deeper

*From the Commentary*

There are at least three reasons why God called Abraham and Sarah. In His love, God was concerned about their salvation; so He revealed His glory and shared His gracious promises. But even beyond their personal salvation was God's purpose in blessing the whole world. This was accomplished when God sent His Son into the world through the Jewish nation. Christ died for the sins of the world (1 John 2:2; 4:14) and wants His church to tell the good news to the whole world (Mark 16:15).

But there is a third reason: The life of Abraham is an example for all Christians who want to walk by faith. Abraham was saved by faith (Gen. 15:6; Rom. 4:1–5; Gal. 3:6–14) and lived by faith (Heb. 11:8–19), and his obedience was the evidence of his faith (James 2:14–26). Abraham obeyed when he did not know *where* (Heb. 11:8–10), *how* (vv. 11–12), *when* (vv. 13–16), or *why* (vv. 17–19); and so should we.

—*Be Obedient*, pages 21–22

3. What are some possible reactions a person could have to being told "all peoples on earth will be blessed through you" (Gen. 12:3)? What might Abraham have expected this blessing to look like? In what sort of time frame? How did Abraham live by faith? What does living by faith look like today?

*From the Commentary*

> Faith is not based on feeling, though the emotions are
> certainly involved (Heb. 11:7). True faith is based on the
> Word of God (Rom. 10:17). God spoke to Abraham and
> told him what He would do *for* him and *through* him
> if he would trust and obey. "Great lives are trained by
> great promises," wrote Joseph Parker, and this was cer-
> tainly true of Abraham and Sarah. God's covenant gave
> them the faith and strength they needed for their lifelong
> pilgrim journey.
>
> —*Be Obedient*, page 22

4. Review Genesis 12:1–3. What's the difference between making promises
to God and believing God's promises to us? What was Abraham's response
to God's call? (See Heb. 11:8–10.) How does our response to God determine
our path?

## From the Commentary

First steps of faith are not always giant steps, which explains why Abraham did not fully obey God. Instead of leaving his family, as he was commanded, Abraham took his father and his nephew Lot with him when he left Ur, and then he stayed at Haran until his father died.

Whatever you bring with you from the old life into the new is likely to create problems. Terah, Abraham's father, kept Abraham from fully obeying the Lord, and Lot created serious problems for Abraham until they finally had to agree to part. Abraham and Sarah brought a sinful agreement with them from Ur (Gen. 20:13), and it got them into trouble twice (12:10–20; 20:1–18).

The life of faith demands total separation *from* what is evil and total devotion *to* what is holy (2 Cor. 6:14—7:1). As you study the life of Abraham, you will discover that he was often tempted to compromise, and occasionally he yielded. God tests us in order to build our faith and bring out the best in us, but the Devil tempts us in order to destroy our faith and bring out the worst in us.

—*Be Obedient*, page 24

5. Review Genesis 11:27–32 and 12:4. What are the practical steps for walking by faith? What evidence do we see in the life of a person who is walking by faith? What are our priorities when we choose to walk by faith? (See also Luke 14:25–27; Isa. 51:1–2.)

*From the Commentary*

In the pilgrim life, you must go "from faith to faith" (Rom. 1:17) if you would go "from strength to strength" (Ps. 84:7). G. A. Studdert Kennedy said, "Faith is not believing in spite of evidence; it is obeying in spite of consequence." "By faith Abraham … obeyed" (Heb. 11:8). Faith without obedience is dead (James 2:14–26), and action without faith is sin (Rom. 14:23). God has wedded faith and obedience like the two sides of a coin; they go together.

This does not mean that sinners are saved by faith plus works, because Scripture declares that sinners are saved by faith alone (John 3:16–18; Eph. 2:8–9). Dr. H. A. Ironside, longtime pastor of Chicago's Moody Church, was told by a woman that she expected to get to heaven by faith plus her good works. "It's like rowing a boat," she explained. "It takes two oars to row a boat; otherwise you go around in a circle."

Dr. Ironside replied, "That's a good illustration except for one thing: *I'm not going to heaven in a rowboat!*"

—*Be Obedient*, pages 27–28

6. How does faith prove itself in good works? (See Eph. 2:8–10; Titus 2:14; 3:8, 14.) What are some of the tests of faith and obedience that Abraham faced? What are some of the tests that believers face today?

## From the Commentary

> In leaving his family and traveling to an unknown land,
> Abraham took a great step of faith. After he arrived, he
> saw God a second time and heard His word of promise.
> Abraham and Sarah probably expected to settle down
> and enjoy their new home, but God would not let them.
> Instead, God permitted a famine to come to the land.
> There is no record that Abraham ever faced a famine in
> Ur or Haran, but now that he was in God's land, he had
> to find food for a large company of people, plus flocks and
> herds (Gen. 14:14).
>
> *—Be Obedient*, pages 31–32

7. Why did God allow the famine? How is this an example of the principle "tests often follow triumphs"? What are other examples of this? (See Ex. 12—17.) How does this principle play out in the church today?

*From the Commentary*

Once in Egypt, Abraham faced a new set of problems, for if you run away from one test, you will soon face another. Once you enroll in the "school of faith," you are not allowed to "drop out" just because of one failure. God has purposes to fulfill in you and through you, and He will do all that is necessary to make you succeed (Ps. 138:8; Phil. 1:6).

In Canaan, all Abraham had to deal with was a famine, but in Egypt, he had to get along with a proud ruler and his officers. Pharaoh was looked on as a god, but he was not a god like Abraham's God, loving and generous and faithful. Abraham soon discovered that he had been better off dealing with the circumstances in Canaan than with the people in Egypt.

—*Be Obedient*, pages 33–34

8. Review Genesis 12:11—13:4. How did Abraham move from trusting to scheming? From confidence to fear? From "other-minded" to selfish? From bringing blessing to bringing judgment? What caused these changes? Where was God in these circumstances?

*More to Consider: Abraham learned his lesson, repented, and left Egypt (Gen. 13:1). What does 1 John 1:9 tell us about the right way to respond after we've disobeyed God's will? What does the opportunity God gives us for a new beginning teach us about His character?*

## From the Commentary

I wonder how many family fights have been caused by the love of money. The newspapers often publish reports about families battling in court because of an inheritance or a lottery winning. People who used to love each other and enjoy each other start attacking each other just to get money, *but money cannot buy the blessings that families freely give.*

Abraham may have failed the first two tests, but he passed this third test with great success.

—*Be Obedient*, page 36

9. Review Genesis 13:5–18. What was the test Abraham faced in this passage? How is this similar to the kinds of tests many Christians face today? How did Abraham respond? What lesson(s) can we take from his response?

## From the Commentary

Not only did Abraham lift up his eyes and look (Gen. 13:14) and lift up his feet and walk (v. 17), but he also lifted up his heart and worshipped God and thanked Him for His gracious blessing. He pitched his tent from place to place as God led him, and he built his altar of witness and worship. The people in Sodom were proud of their affluence (Ezek. 16:49), but Abraham had spiritual wealth that they knew nothing about. He was walking in fellowship with God, and his heart was satisfied.

—*Be Obedient*, pages 39–40

10. What did spiritual wealth look like in Abraham's economy? What does it look like in the church today? How is spiritual wealth measured?

## Looking Inward

Take a moment to reflect on all that you've explored thus far in this study of Genesis 11:27—13:18. Review your notes and answers and think about how each of these things matters in your life today.

*Tips for Small Groups: To get the most out of this section, form pairs or trios and have group members take turns answering these questions. Be honest and as open as you can in this discussion, but most of all, be encouraging and supportive of others. Be sensitive to those who are going through particularly difficult times and don't press for people to speak if they're uncomfortable doing so.*

11. What are some ways you feel called by God? What has God called you to do? How have you responded?

12. What does it mean to you to live by faith? What are the greatest roadblocks to living by faith? How easy or difficult is it for you to live by faith?

13. Have you ever experienced the "tests often follow triumphs" principle? Explain. How did you deal with the tests that followed? What lessons did you learn about yourself in this season? What did you learn about God?

## Going Forward

14. Think of one or two things that you have learned that you'd like to work on in the coming week. Remember that this is all about quality, not quantity. It's better to work on one specific area of life and do it well than to work on many and do poorly (or to be so overwhelmed that you simply don't try).

Do you need to grow your faith? Do you need to deal obediently with a particular test? Be specific. Go back through Genesis 11:27—13:18 and put a star next to the phrase or verse that is most encouraging to you. Consider memorizing this verse.

*Real-Life Application Ideas: Abraham faced many tests in his life. Some of these he passed with flying colors; others he struggled with. Take inventory of some of the things you've faced in your faith life. Note the tests you're facing today. What have you learned about faith from the way you responded to past tests? How can you apply those lessons to what you're facing today? Spend some time in prayer, focusing specifically on seeking God's wisdom for the tests you're facing and asking Him for a greater portion of faith to deal with those tests.*

## Seeking Help

15. Write a prayer below (or simply pray one in silence), inviting God to work on your mind and heart in those areas you've noted in the Going Forward section. Be honest about your desires and fears.

*Notes for Small Groups:*
- *Look for ways to put into practice the things you wrote in the Going Forward section. Talk with other group members about your ideas and commit to being accountable to one another.*
- *During the coming week, ask the Holy Spirit to continue to reveal truth to you from what you've read and studied.*
- *Before you start the next lesson, read Genesis 14. For more in-depth lesson preparation, read chapter 3, "Faith Is the Victory," in* Be Obedient.

# Faith
## (GENESIS 14)

*Before you begin ...*
- *Pray for the Holy Spirit to reveal truth and wisdom as you go through this lesson.*
- *Read Genesis 14. This lesson references chapter 3 in* Be Obedient. *It will be helpful for you to have your Bible and a copy of the commentary available as you work through this lesson.*

## Getting Started

### From the Commentary

When you walk in the light (1 John 1:5–10), you can see what is going on, and you experience variety in your life. But in the darkness, everything looks alike. No wonder unsaved people (and backslidden believers) are so bored and must constantly seek escape! The life of faith presents challenges that keep you going—and keep you growing!

In Genesis 14, Abraham, the man of faith, fulfills three special roles: the watcher (vv. 1–12), the warrior (vv. 13–16), and the worshipper (vv. 17–24). In all three roles, Abraham exercised faith in God and made the right decisions.

—*Be Obedient*, pages 43–44

1. Review the three roles noted in the previous commentary excerpt. How did Abraham exercise faith in each circumstance? What would have been the wrong decisions in each case? How did he know right from wrong in each role?

*More to Consider: God wants us to mature in every area of life, but maturity doesn't come easily. There can be no growth without challenge, and there can be no challenge without change. If circumstances never changed, everything would be predictable, and the more predictable life becomes, the less challenge it presents. William Cullen Bryant wrote, "Weep not that the world changes—did it keep / A stable changeless state, 'twere cause indeed to weep." What is it about change that frightens believers? How was Abraham's response to change a model for all God followers?*

2. Choose one verse or phrase from Genesis 14 that stands out to you. This could be something you're intrigued by, something that makes you uncomfortable, something that puzzles you, something that resonates with you, or just something you want to examine further. Write that here.

# Going Deeper

*From the Commentary*

Genesis 14:1–12 records the first war mentioned in the Bible, and it would not be included here had it not involved Abraham. The Bible records a great deal of history, but as Dr. A. T. Pierson said, "History is His story." What is written helps us better understand how God worked out His great plan of salvation in this world. In the Bible, historical facts are often windows for spiritual truth.

The five city-states in the plain of Jordan (Gen. 14:2; see also 13:10) had been subject for twelve years to the kings of four eastern city-states (14:1) and finally revolted against them. This, of course, was a declaration of war; so the four kings invaded the plain of Jordan to bring the five kings into subjection. From our modern viewpoint, the invasion was a minor skirmish, but in that day, it was considered a major international conflict.

Certainly five kings ought to be able to defeat four kings, especially when they are fighting "on their own turf." But the army of the cities of the plain was soundly defeated by the invading kings! Apparently the five kings did not even know their own land because they were trapped in the slime pits (v. 10). All their army could do was flee for the hills.

—*Be Obedient*, page 44

3. What was the core cause of the war mentioned in Genesis 14:1–12? What was Abraham's role in this? What does this reveal to us about the cause of war in general? About God's response to war?

## From the Commentary

While in Egypt with Abraham, Lot had gotten a taste of the world and enjoyed it. Scripture doesn't record that Lot ever built an altar and sought the Lord, as did his uncle Abraham. Abraham was the friend of God (James 2:23), but Lot was the friend of the world (4:4). In time, Lot conformed to the world (Rom. 12:2), and when Sodom lost the war, Lot was condemned with the world (1 Cor. 11:32). If you identify with the world, then expect to suffer what the world suffers.

—*Be Obedient*, page 45

4. What did Lot's capture reveal about God's character? About God's hope for His people? What is the message here for today's church?

## From the History Books

The Bible is packed with details about wars and skirmishes between nations and neighbors. From the very first mention of war in Genesis to the last one in Revelation, God's role is clear: He works out the results according to His plan. In the centuries since Jesus' birth, wars have continued to rage—even now they continue around the world. In most cases wars seem to be about land, but they are equally about religious beliefs—certainty that God is on one side or the other leads to disagreement and then to destruction.

5. What is different between the wars described in the Bible and the ones that have occurred since? How do we determine God's will in war? Why are the battles so often about land or religious beliefs? What can we state

with certainty about God's plan in relation to the wars our world has faced in recent years?

## From the Commentary

Abraham did not get involved in the war until he heard that Lot had been captured, and then he began to act. *Abraham was separated, but not isolated; he was independent, but not indifferent.* In fact, he and some of the local sheiks had formed an alliance for just such emergencies (Gen. 14:13). He was "Abram the Hebrew" (v. 13), which means "the outsider, the person with no secure place in society." He was not "Abraham the hard-hearted." He was a "pilgrim and stranger" in the land, but that was no excuse for inaction.

While believers must not compromise with the unsaved in matters of spiritual walk and ministry (2 Cor. 6:14—7:1), they may cooperate when it comes to caring for humanity and "promoting the general welfare." When you see that people are in trouble, you don't ask them for a testimony before helping them (Luke 10:25–37; Gal. 6:10). Sacrificial service is one way of showing the love of Christ to others (Matt. 5:16). If Christians don't carry their share of the common burdens of life, how can they be the salt of the earth and the light of the world?

*—Be Obedient*, pages 45–46

6. Review Genesis 14:13–16. Respond to the claim that "Abraham was separated, but not isolated; he was independent, but not indifferent" regarding the war. How might this apply to us today? What are some of the common burdens Christians ought to share in carrying today? How do we do that without compromising our beliefs?

## From the Commentary

Abraham treated his nephew with love, both when he gave Lot first choice of the land (Gen. 13:9) and when he risked his own life to rescue him. Lot had not been kind to Abraham, and Abraham had every excuse to let his nephew suffer the painful consequences of his own stupid decisions. But Lot was his "brother" (14:16), so Abraham practiced brotherly love and overcame evil with good.

*—Be Obedient*, page 46

7. Read Romans 12:17–21 and Galatians 6:1–2. How do these verses apply to the way Abraham treated his nephew? What was his example of brotherly love? What does this love look like in today's church?

## From the Commentary

When you consider the characteristics of Abraham's army, you see what it takes in the spiritual realm to have victory over the world.

(1) They were born in his house.

(2) They were armed.

(3) They were trained.

(4) They believed in their leader.

(5) They were united.

(6) They were single-minded.

—*Be Obedient*, pages 46–48

8. Review the six attributes of Abraham's army as listed in the previous commentary excerpt. Why is each of these attributes important? What are some of the applications of this today?

*More to Consider: "No one serving as a soldier gets involved in civilian affairs—he wants to please his commanding officer" (2 Tim. 2:4). Read about Achan (Josh. 7), Samson (Judg. 13—16), and Saul (1 Sam. 15). How do these stories reveal the truth of the statement in 2 Timothy?*

### From the Commentary

Sometimes you face your greatest dangers after you have won a battle. It was after the capture of Jericho that Israel's self-confidence led it into defeat at Ai (Josh. 7), and after his success on Mount Carmel, Elijah panicked and ran away in fear (1 Kings 19). No wonder the saintly Scottish pastor Andrew Bonar (1810–1892) said, "Let us be as watchful after the victory as before the battle."

When Abraham returned from battle, he was met by two kings: Bera, king of Sodom ("burning"), and Melchizedek, king of Salem ("peace"). Bera offered Abraham all the spoils in return for the people, while Melchizedek gave Abraham bread and wine. Abraham rejected Bera's offer but accepted the bread and wine from Melchizedek and gave him tithes of the spoils. All of this is symbolic and presents some important spiritual truths that you should understand and apply today.

Abraham had to choose between two kings who represented two opposite ways of life. Sodom was a wicked city (Gen. 13:13; Ezek. 16:49–50), and Bera represented the dominion of this world system with its appeal to the flesh (Eph. 2:1–3). Bera means "gift," suggesting that the world bargains for your allegiance. But Sodom means "burning," so be careful how you choose!

*—Be Obedient*, page 49

9. Review Genesis 14:17–24. What led Abraham to reject Bera's offer? Why did he so readily accept Melchizedek's? What is the lesson for us today in this little story?

## From the Commentary

Melchizedek had something better to offer Abraham: the blessing of the "Most High God, possessor of heaven and earth." *Abraham lived by the blessing of the Lord, not by the bribery of the world.* He did not want anybody to think that the world made him rich. Even a small thing like a shoelace might affect his walk! Too many servants of God have weakened their testimonies by accepting applause and gifts from the people of the world. You cannot be a servant of God and a celebrity in the world at the same time.

—*Be Obedient*, page 50

10. Why is it so tempting to accept applause and gifts from the world? In what ways might Abraham have been tempted by these? How was he able to resist? What are some prevalent temptations today? How can God help us resist them?

# Looking Inward

Take a moment to reflect on all that you've explored thus far in this study of Genesis 14. Review your notes and answers and think about how each of these things matters in your life today.

*Tips for Small Groups: To get the most out of this section, form pairs or trios and have group members take turns answering these questions. Be honest and as open as you can in this discussion, but most of all, be encouraging and supportive of others. Be sensitive to those who are going through particularly difficult times and don't press for people to speak if they're uncomfortable doing so.*

11. What are some of the battles you've experienced in life? How did you approach them? What role (if any) did your faith in God play in these scenarios? If you didn't trust God, what did you do?

12. How do you feel about the recent wars our world has faced (and is still facing)? Where is God in the middle of each of those wars? What is your responsibility in times of war? What are your greatest challenges?

13. When have you made a mistake or bad decision because of too much self-confidence? What role did pride play in that situation? What role does (or should) humility play in the lives of believers who've just experienced some kind of victory?

## Going Forward

14. Think of one or two things that you have learned that you'd like to work on in the coming week. Remember that this is all about quality, not quantity. It's better to work on one specific area of life and do it well than to work on many and do poorly (or to be so overwhelmed that you simply don't try).

Do you need to choose between the world and God's ways? Be specific. Go back through Genesis 14 and put a star next to the phrase or verse that is most encouraging to you. Consider memorizing this verse.

*Real-Life Application Ideas: Whatever your personal beliefs are about the wars and battles that rage around the world today, there is little argument that the people involved in those battles could use hope and encouragement. Take time this week to reach out to soldiers or family members of soldiers, offering time, care, concern, and any practical needs you can. Don't focus on the controversy or challenge the reasons for the war; just be Jesus to them and offer love. Meanwhile, continue to seek God's will and ask for His peace to blanket the land.*

## Seeking Help

15. Write a prayer below (or simply pray one in silence), inviting God to work on your mind and heart in those areas you've noted in the Going Forward section. Be honest about your desires and fears.

*Notes for Small Groups:*

- *Look for ways to put into practice the things you wrote in the Going Forward section. Talk with other group members about your ideas and commit to being accountable to one another.*

- *During the coming week, ask the Holy Spirit to continue to reveal truth to you from what you've read and studied.*

- *Before you start the next lesson, read Genesis 15. For more in-depth lesson preparation, read chapter 4, "The Dark Night of the Soul," in* Be Obedient.

#  The Dark Night
## (GENESIS 15)

*Before you begin …*

- *Pray for the Holy Spirit to reveal truth and wisdom as you go through this lesson.*
- *Read Genesis 15. This lesson references chapter 4 in* Be Obedient. *It will be helpful for you to have your Bible and a copy of the commentary available as you work through this lesson.*

## Getting Started

### From the Commentary

> "One who truly fears God, and is obedient to Him, may be in a condition of darkness, and have no light; and he may walk many days and years in that condition."

So wrote the Puritan divine Thomas Goodwin (1600–1679), and the prophet Isaiah agrees with him: "Who among you fears the LORD? Who obeys the voice of His Servant? Who walks in darkness and has no light? Let him trust in the name of the LORD and rely upon his God" (Isa. 50:10 NKJV).

At times even the most dedicated Christian feels "in the dark" and wonders why God seems so far away. During the Boxer Rebellion, the China Inland Mission suffered greatly, and its founder, J. Hudson Taylor, said to a friend, "I cannot read; I cannot think; I cannot even pray; but I can trust." It was a dark time, but God eventually gave light.

Abraham had an experience of what spiritual directors call "the dark night of the soul." The term comes from a sixteenth-century spiritual classic of that title by St. John of the Cross. Based on the night scenes described in the Song of Songs, the book tells how the child of God enters into deeper love and faith by experiencing temporary darkness and seeming separation from God. It is not an easy thing to experience, but sometimes necessary.

—*Be Obedient*, page 57

1. What prompted Abraham's dark night? Why is such a thing sometimes necessary? How did it affect Abraham?

2. Choose one verse or phrase from Genesis 15 that stands out to you. This could be something you're intrigued by, something that makes you uncomfortable, something that puzzles you, something that resonates with you, or just something you want to examine further. Write that here.

## Going Deeper

*From the Commentary*

> The previous chapter focused on Abraham's actions, but chapter 15 deals with his emotions, including the "horror of great darkness" (Gen. 15:12). People with faith are also people with feelings, and feelings must not be discredited or ignored. Many orthodox Christians are prone to emphasize the mind and will and minimize the emotions, but this is a grave error that can lead to an unbalanced life.
>
> You certainly ought to "listen to your feelings" and be honest about them. "When a person assumes responsibility for his feelings," writes psychiatrist David Viscott, "he assumes responsibility for his world." But don't stop there: Take time to listen to God and receive His words of encouragement. This is the first time in the Bible you find

the phrase *the word of the Lord came;* it is used more than one hundred times in the Old Testament. The faith that conquers fear is faith in the Word, not faith in feelings.

This is also the first time you find the assuring words *fear not* in the Bible. God repeated them to Isaac (Gen. 26:24) and Jacob (46:3) and often to the people of Israel (Ex. 14:13; 20:20; Num. 14:9; Deut. 1:21). The "fear not" promises in Isaiah are good to read and ponder when you find yourself dealing with fear (Isa. 41:10, 13–14; 43:1, 5; 44:2, 8).

—*Be Obedient*, pages 58–59

3. What is the danger of ignoring feelings? Of ignoring wisdom or intelligence? What does it look like to trust God with both? Why is it significant that the words *fear not* appear in this chapter of Genesis?

*More to Consider: Now that the battle was won, why would Abraham be afraid? For one thing, he was human, and our emotions can fall apart after a time of great danger and difficulty. Review 1 Kings 19. How does Abraham's example explain why Elijah was so discouraged after the victory over Baal on Mount Carmel?*

## From the Commentary

God's remedy for Abraham's fear was to remind him who He was: "I am thy shield, and thy exceeding great reward" (Gen. 15:1). God's I AM is perfectly adequate for man's "I am not." "Be still, and know that I am God" (Ps. 46:10). Your life is only as big as your faith, and your faith is only as big as your God. If you spend all your time looking at yourself, you will get discouraged, but if you look to God by faith, you will be encouraged.

God is our shield and our reward, our protection and our provision. Abraham didn't have to worry about another battle because the Lord would protect him. And he didn't need to regret losing the wealth offered him by the king of Sodom because God would reward him in far greater ways.

—*Be Obedient*, page 59

4. Read Matthew 6:33 and Philippians 4:19. How is the message in Genesis 15 similar to these passages? What did it mean to Abraham that God was his shield, protection, and provision? What does it mean to the church today?

## From Today's World

Protection and provision are blessings that the world is seeking and politicians are promising whenever they run for office. Candidates offer voters protection from war and danger on the streets as well as provision for jobs, health care, education, and retirement. These promises are often at the core of a politician's election strategy. However, in practice (in part because of the challenges inherent in political office) such promises are often impossible to keep.

5. Why do politicians focus on themes like provision and protection in their campaign speeches? Why do these appeal to the voting public? What does Abraham's story teach us about the only true way to find provision and protection? (See Ps. 84:11.)

## From the Commentary

God had promised Abraham that his descendants would be as numerous as the dust of the earth (Gen. 13:16) and that they would bring blessing to the whole world (12:1–3). But Abraham and Sarah were still childless, and if Abraham died, the only heir he had was his "chief of staff"—Eliezer. (He may be the servant mentioned in 24:2.) Lot was no longer in the picture, and Abraham's other relatives were five hundred miles away in Mesopotamia. What had happened to the promise?

Abraham's concern was not just for himself and his wife, though like all Eastern couples, they wanted children. His concern was for the working out of God's plan of salvation for the whole world. God had a glorious plan, and God made a gracious promise, *but God seemed to be doing nothing!* Abraham and Sarah were getting older, and time was running out.

—*Be Obedient*, page 60

6. Review Genesis 15:2–3. Why was Abraham losing patience with God? What does this story teach us about God's timing? About our ability to wait on God? What are some of the things the church today is "waiting" on?

## From the Commentary

One of the basic lessons in the "school of faith" is: *God's will must be fulfilled in God's way and in God's time.* God did not expect Abraham and Sarah to figure out how to have an heir; all He asked was that they be available so He could accomplish His purposes in and through them. What Abraham and Sarah did not realize was that God was waiting for them to be "as good as dead" so that God alone would receive the glory.

It is good to share your concerns with the Lord, even if what you say seems to evidence unbelief or impatience in your heart. God is not deaf to your questions or unconcerned about your feelings. He did not rebuke Abraham; instead, He gave him the assurances that he needed.

—*Be Obedient*, pages 60–61

7. What are some ways Abraham and Sarah expressed their concerns with God? What was God's response? What are the assurances God gives us today? (See 1 Peter 5:7.)

*From the Commentary*

Promises do us no good unless we believe them and act on them. Abraham had already trusted God's promise

(Gen. 12:1–3) and proved it by leaving home and going to Canaan (Heb. 11:8). But Genesis 15:6 is the first reference in the Bible to Abraham's faith. It is the John 3:16 of the Old Testament, and for this reason, the New Testament writers use it to illustrate salvation by faith.

There are only five words in the Hebrew original of Genesis 15:6, but what a wealth of meaning they contain.

—*Be Obedient*, page 61

8. Review Genesis 15:6. Then read Galatians 3:6; Romans 4:3; and James 2:23. Why are these words quoted so often in the New Testament? What does this reveal to us about their importance?

*More to Consider: Read Galatians 3; Romans 4; and James 2. How do these chapters reveal the truth of Genesis 15:6? What does it tell us about this verse that it takes three New Testament chapters to explain it?*

## From the Commentary

> In Genesis 15:7, God reaffirmed the promise to Abraham that He would give the land of Canaan to him and his descendants (Gen. 12:7; 13:15, 17). The land is an important part of the covenant, for it is in the land of Israel that the divine drama of "salvation history" was enacted. The land of Israel will also be the stage for the final act of that drama when the Messiah returns to reign on earth.
>
> For centuries, Israel was a nation without a land, and it seemed that the covenant promises would not be fulfilled. In 1932, British expositor G. Campbell Morgan wrote, "I am now quite convinced that the teaching of Scripture as a whole is that there is no future for Israel as an earthly people at all" (*This Was His Faith*, 290). Then came May 14, 1948, and the rebirth of national Israel! Just as God kept His promise to Abraham and sent the Messiah, so He will keep His promise and restore the land to His people.
>
> —*Be Obedient*, page 63

9. Why was this promise of land so important to the nation of Israel? How does the promise continue to affect the Jews today? What implications does it have for the ongoing conflict in the Middle East?

*From the Commentary*

At the beginning of Abraham's pilgrimage, God said to him, "I will show thee" the land (Gen. 12:1). Later He said, "I will give it unto thee" (13:15–17). But now His word is, "To your descendants I have given this land" (15:18 NASB). God's covenant made it a settled matter: The land belongs to Abraham's descendants through Isaac.

Solomon exercised dominion over a vast area (1 Kings 4:21; Ps. 72:8), but Israel did not *possess* all that land. The kings merely acknowledged Solomon's sovereignty and paid tribute to him. When Jesus Christ reigns from the throne of David (Matt. 19:28; Luke 1:32), the land of Israel will reach the full dimensions promised by God.

God's covenant with Abraham stands no matter what Israel believes. The covenant is unconditional; its fulfillment does not depend on man's faith or faithfulness. In like manner, the new covenant established by Jesus Christ is dependable whether people accept it or not.

—*Be Obedient*, page 65

10. Read Hebrews 5:9; 9:12, 15; and 1 Peter 5:10. What do these verses tell us about those who place their faith in Jesus and enter into His covenant? Review Genesis 15:8–21. What does this passage teach us about God's covenants? What does it mean that God's covenant stands no matter what people believe? Why is this relevant to Israel? To Christians today?

## Looking Inward

Take a moment to reflect on all that you've explored thus far in this study of Genesis 15. Review your notes and answers and think about how each of these things matters in your life today.

*Tips for Small Groups: To get the most out of this section, form pairs or trios and have group members take turns answering these questions. Be honest and as open as you can in this discussion, but most of all, be encouraging and supportive of others. Be sensitive to those who are going through particularly difficult times and don't press for people to speak if they're uncomfortable doing so.*

11. Have you experienced a "dark night of the soul"? Describe that time. What led you to that place? What was it like in the midst of it? How did you find your way out? If you're still there, what can you do to move toward God's light?

12. Do you tend to trust your intellect or your emotions more? Explain. How does God show up in your emotional life? In your intellectual life? How do you find a proper balance between these two?

13. What are some questions you're waiting impatiently for God to answer? Why do you think He is taking His time in dealing with those circumstances? What is the right way to wait on God? How is waiting on God an active thing?

## Going Forward

14. Think of one or two things that you have learned that you'd like to work on in the coming week. Remember that this is all about quality, not quantity. It's better to work on one specific area of life and do it well than to work on many and do poorly (or to be so overwhelmed that you simply don't try).

Do you need to learn how to wait on God? Be specific. Go back through Genesis 15 and put a star next to the phrase or verse that is most encouraging to you. Consider memorizing this verse.

*Real-Life Application Ideas: It's highly likely that one or more people you know (or perhaps it's you) is experiencing a "dark night of the soul." There is little a person can do for someone suffering from this doubt and loneliness, but often the simple act of being a listener is enough to shine a small light into the darkness. Listen for clues to find out if anyone you know or care about is in that place. Then offer your ears to hear his or her ache. Don't use the time to judge or offer easy solutions to the pain. Just listen and pray. Let God do the rest.*

## Seeking Help

15. Write a prayer below (or simply pray one in silence), inviting God to work on your mind and heart in those areas you've noted in the Going Forward section. Be honest about your desires and fears.

*Notes for Small Groups:*

- *Look for ways to put into practice the things you wrote in the Going Forward section. Talk with other group members about your ideas and commit to being accountable to one another.*

- *During the coming week, ask the Holy Spirit to continue to reveal truth to you from what you've read and studied.*

- *Before you start the next lesson, read Genesis 16—17. For more in-depth lesson preparation, read chapters 5 and 6, "Beware of Detours!" and "What's in a Name?" in* Be Obedient.

# Detours and Names

## (GENESIS 16—17)

*Before you begin ...*
- *Pray for the Holy Spirit to reveal truth and wisdom as you go through this lesson.*
- *Read Genesis 16—17. This lesson references chapters 5 and 6 in* Be Obedient. *It will be helpful for you to have your Bible and a copy of the commentary available as you work through this lesson.*

## Getting Started

### From the Commentary

Genesis 16 records a painful detour that Abraham and Sarah made in their pilgrim walk, a detour that brought conflict not only into their home but also into the world. What today's journalists call "the Arab-Israeli conflict" began right here.

But this account is much more than ancient history with modern consequences. It's a good lesson for God's people about walking by faith and waiting for God to fulfill His promises in His way and in His time. As you study the stages in the experience of Abraham and Sarah, you will see how dangerous it is to depend on your own wisdom.

—*Be Obedient*, pages 69–70

1. In what ways did Abraham trust in his own wisdom instead of listening to God? Why did he make this decision? What are examples of this kind of impatience in the church today? How do we embrace both urgency and patience in our faith lives?

*More to Consider: Why do you think God waited so long to fulfill His promise to Abraham? (See Heb. 11:12; Rom. 4:20.) What does this teach us about how God acts today?*

2. Choose one verse or phrase from Genesis 16—17 that stands out to you. This could be something you're intrigued by, something that makes you uncomfortable, something that puzzles you, something that resonates with you, or just something you want to examine further. Write that here.

# Going Deeper

*From the Commentary*

> These are the evidences of true biblical faith: (1) you are concerned only for the glory of God; (2) you are willing to wait; (3) you are obeying God's Word; and (4) you have God's joy and peace within. While Abraham and Sarah were waiting, God was increasing their faith and patience and building character (James 1:1–4). Then something happened that put Abraham and Sarah on a painful detour.
>
> —*Be Obedient*, page 71

3. Review the four evidences of biblical faith as noted in the previous commentary excerpt. How did Abraham fulfill these? How did he neglect them? Does waiting on God always mean God is increasing faith or building character? What are other results of (or reasons for) waiting on God?

## From the Commentary

Sarah knew that she was incapable of bearing a child but that her husband was still capable of begetting a child. God had specifically named Abraham as the father of the promised heir, *but He had not yet identified the mother*. Logically, it would be Abraham's wife, but perhaps God had other plans. Sarah was "second-guessing" God, and this is a dangerous thing to do. Remember, true faith is based on the Word of God (Rom. 10:17) and not on the wisdom of man (Prov. 3:5–6) because "faith is living without scheming." Sarah said, "It may be"; she did not say, "Thus saith the Lord!" God had told Abraham, "Know of a surety" (Gen. 15:13), but Sarah had no such assurance on which to base her actions.

Furthermore, Sarah was not concerned about the glory of God; her only goal was "that I may obtain children by her" (Gen. 16:2). Perhaps there is a hint of disappointment with God and even *blaming* God when she says, "The LORD hath restrained me from bearing" (v. 2).

—*Be Obedient*, page 71

4. What does Sarah's response to God's promise teach us about the way Satan speaks to God's people? What does it say about Sarah that she second-guessed God? What are ways today's believers second-guess God?

*From the Commentary*

Of all fights, family fights are the most painful and the most difficult to settle. Had Hagar maintained the attitude of a servant, things might have been different, but she became proud, and this irritated her mistress (Prov. 30:21–23).

"Having begun in the Spirit, are ye now made perfect by the flesh?" Paul asked (Gal. 3:3), and you see this illustrated in Abraham's home. He and Sarah had begun in the Spirit when they put their faith in the Lord, but now they had turned to the flesh for help, and some of the works of the flesh were starting to appear (Gal. 5:19–21). Abraham, Sarah, and Hagar were at war with one another because they were at war with the Lord, and they were at war with the Lord because they had selfish desires warring within their own hearts (James 4:1–10).

The first thing they should have done was build an altar, worship the Lord, and tell Him their problems. They should have confessed their sins and received His gracious forgiveness. Once you stop fighting with God and with yourself, you will have an easier time not fighting with others. The first step toward reconciliation with others is getting right with God.

However, instead of facing their sins honestly, each of the persons involved took a different course, and this only made things worse.

—*Be Obedient*, pages 72–73

5. Review Genesis 16:4–6. How does James 3:13–18 speak to this situation? Why do people so quickly point blame at others when they're the ones responsible? What does this say about their relationships with God?

## From the Commentary

Genesis 16:7–14 records the first appearance in Scripture of the Angel of the Lord, who is generally identified as our Lord Jesus Christ. In Genesis 16:10, the angel promised to do what only God can do, and in verse 13, Hagar called the angel "God." These preincarnation visits of Jesus Christ to the earth were to meet special needs and to accomplish special tasks. The fact that the Son of God took on a temporary body, left heaven, and came down to help a rejected servant-girl surely reveals His grace and love. His servants Abraham and Sarah had sinned against the Lord and against Hagar, but the Lord did not desert them.

The angel called her "Sarah's maid," which suggests that God did not accept her marriage to Abraham. Apparently Hagar was on her way back to Egypt when she met the angel, but God told her to return to Abraham's camp and submit herself to her mistress. That would take a great deal of faith, because Sarah had mistreated Hagar before and might do it again.

God then told her that she was pregnant with a son, whom she should name Ishmael ("God hears"). While he would not be Abraham's heir in the blessings of the covenant, Ishmael would still enjoy blessings from God because he was Abraham's son. God promised to multiply Ishmael's descendants and make them into great nations (Gen. 21:18; 25:12–18), and He did, for Ishmael is the founder of the Arab peoples.

Hagar did return and submit herself to Sarah. Surely she apologized for being arrogant, for despising her mistress, and for running away. She trusted God to protect her and her son and to care for them in the years to come. We never solve life's problems by running away. Submit to God and trust Him to work things out for your good and His glory.

—*Be Obedient*, pages 74–75

6. What is significant about the first appearance of the Angel of the Lord? Why would God choose to show up in this way to Hagar, considering the circumstances of Hagar's story? What does this reveal to us about God's ways? About how God moved His plan for salvation forward?

## From the Commentary

> Genesis 17:1–2 is the first time the Hebrew name *El Shaddai* (shuh-DYE) occurs in Scripture. *Shaddai* is translated as "Almighty" forty-eight times in the Old Testament. In the New Testament, the Greek equivalent is used in 2 Corinthians 6:18 and Revelation 1:8; 4:8; 11:17; 15:3; 16:7 and 14; 19:6 and 15; and 21:22. It is translated "Almighty" except in Revelation 19:6 ("omnipotent").
>
> *El* is the name of God that speaks of power; but what does *Shaddai* mean? Scholars do not agree. Some say it comes from a Hebrew word meaning "to be strong"; others prefer a word meaning "mountain" or "breast." Metaphorically, a mountain is a "breast" that rises up from the plain, and certainly a mountain is a symbol of strength. If we combine these several ideas, we might say that *El Shaddai* is the name of "the all-powerful and all-sufficient God who can do anything and meet any need."
>
> —*Be Obedient*, page 82

7. Review Genesis 17:1–2. Why would God reveal the name *El Shaddai* to Abraham at this time, after thirteen years of silence? What was His message to Abraham? Go through Genesis 17 and underline the uses of the phrase "I will." What does this tell us about God's plan? About God's character?

## From the Commentary

"Abram" means "exalted father"; "Abraham" means "father of a multitude." When Abraham informed the people in his camp that he had a new name, some of them must have smiled and said, "Father of a multitude! Why, he and his wife are too old to have children!" Whether he looked beneath his feet or up into the heavens, or whenever anyone called him by name, Abraham was reminded of God's gracious promise to give him many descendants.

Keep in mind that Abraham's descendants include not only the Jewish people, but also the Arab world (through Ishmael) and the nations listed in Genesis 25:1–4. All who trust Jesus Christ as Savior are spiritual children of Abraham (Gal. 3:6–9), and that will be a vast multitude (Rev. 7:9).

In being fruitful for God, we have nothing in ourselves that will accomplish the task. Abraham and Sarah had tried their own plan, and it failed miserably.

—*Be Obedient*, pages 83–84

8. Read John 15:5. How is this verse applicable to Abraham and Sarah's story? How might the story have played out differently if they'd trusted God instead of trying to take matters into their own hands? How is this same story repeated time and again in biblical history? How is it true in today's church?

*More to Consider: Romans 4:9–12 makes it clear that the physical operation of circumcision had nothing to do with Abraham's eternal salvation. Abraham had believed God and received God's righteousness before he ever was circumcised (Gen. 15:6). Circumcision was not the means of his salvation but the mark of his separation as a man in covenant relationship with God. What does all this mean to Christians today? (See Rom. 8:9, 16; Eph. 1:13; 4:30; Phil. 3:1–3; Col. 2:9–12.)*

## From the Commentary

"Sarah" means "princess." (We are not certain what "Sarai" means. Some say "to mock" or "to be contentious." It could also be another form of the word "princess.") Since she would become the mother of kings, it was only right that she be called a princess!

We must not minimize the place of Sarah in God's great plan of salvation. Like her husband (and all of us), she had her faults, but also like her husband, she trusted God and accomplished His purposes (Heb. 11:11). She is not only the mother of the Jewish nation (Isa. 51:2) but also a good example for Christian wives to follow (1 Peter 3:1–6). The Christian husband should treat his wife like a princess because that is what she is in the Lord.

Three different occasions of laughter are associated with Isaac's birth: Abraham laughed for joy when he heard his wife would give birth to the promised son (Gen. 17:17); Sarah laughed in unbelief when she heard the news

(18:9–15); and Sarah laughed for joy when the boy was born (21:6–7). The name Isaac means "he laughs."

—*Be Obedient*, page 88

9. Why is it important that Sarah received a new name? What does this tell us about God's love for His people, even when they've made poor decisions? Why do you think laughter was so closely associated with Isaac's birth? What does this reveal about God? About what it means to trust God's plan?

*From the Commentary*

The first baby in the Bible who was named before birth was Ishmael (Gen. 16:11), and the second was Isaac. As we shall see when we study Genesis 21, these two boys represent two different births: (1) Ishmael, our first birth after the flesh, and (2) Isaac, our second birth through the Spirit. (See John 3:1–8 and Gal. 4:21–31, especially vv. 28–29.)

From the human point of view, we can understand why Abraham interceded for Ishmael. Ishmael was his son, and the father loved him dearly. They had been together now for thirteen years, and Ishmael was entering adulthood. Was God going to waste all that Abraham had invested in Ishmael? Was there to be no future for the lad? After all, it wasn't Ishmael's fault that he was born! It was Abraham and Sarah who sinned, not the boy.

But from the spiritual point of view, Ishmael could not replace Isaac or even be equal to him in the covenant plan of God. God had already promised to bless Ishmael (Gen. 16:11), and He kept His promise (25:12–16), but the covenant blessings were not a part of Ishmael's heritage. Isaac alone was to be the heir of all things (25:5–6; Rom. 9:6–13).

—*Be Obedient*, page 89

10. Review Genesis 17:18–22. What is the practical lesson in this story for those who seek to live by faith? What does this story teach us about clinging to the past? About trusting in God's plan for the future?

## Looking Inward

Take a moment to reflect on all that you've explored thus far in this study of Genesis 16—17. Review your notes and answers and think about how each of these things matters in your life today.

*Tips for Small Groups: To get the most out of this section, form pairs or trios and have group members take turns answering these questions. Be honest and as open as you can in this discussion, but most of all, be encouraging and supportive of others. Be sensitive to those who are going through particularly difficult times and don't press for people to speak if they're uncomfortable doing so.*

11. What are some of the ways you've second-guessed God? What was the result of your second-guessing? Why is it so hard to wait on God sometimes? Where can you go to find the patience to wait on God?

12. Are you quick to accept responsibility for poor decisions or do you tend to turn the blame on someone else? What is the cost (to yourself, to others, to your relationship with God) when you don't take responsibility? What does it take to reconcile these actions?

13. Are you someone who tends to cling to the past or do you mostly look forward to the future? Explain. Why is it important for your faith that you look forward? What is a good way to consider the past without clinging to it?

## Going Forward

14. Think of one or two things that you have learned that you'd like to work on in the coming week. Remember that this is all about quality, not quantity. It's better to work on one specific area of life and do it well than to work on many and do poorly (or to be so overwhelmed that you simply don't try).

Do you want to stop second-guessing God? Be specific. Go back through Genesis 16—17 and put a star next to the phrase or verse that is most encouraging to you. Consider memorizing this verse.

*Real-Life Application Ideas: Consider the things that you're still hanging onto from the past. Does holding onto these things help you move forward in your relationship with Christ? If not, how can you turn from the past to the future? Take a few minutes to think about all the plans God has for you. Make a list of the things you think He would want you to pursue—regarding family, career, friends, ministry, etc. Then spend time in prayer, asking God to make clear the path you are to take in each of those areas. Work diligently to let go of things that hold you back, allowing God to move you forward.*

## Seeking Help

15. Write a prayer below (or simply pray one in silence), inviting God to work on your mind and heart in those areas you've noted in the Going Forward section. Be honest about your desires and fears.

*Notes for Small Groups:*

- *Look for ways to put into practice the things you wrote in the Going Forward section. Talk with other group members about your ideas and commit to being accountable to one another.*

- *During the coming week, ask the Holy Spirit to continue to reveal truth to you from what you've read and studied.*

- *Before you start the next lesson, read Genesis 18—20. For more in-depth lesson preparation, read chapters 7 and 8, "So As by Fire" and "Abraham the Neighbor," in* Be Obedient.

# By Fire

## (GENESIS 18—20)

*Before you begin …*
- *Pray for the Holy Spirit to reveal truth and wisdom as you go through this lesson.*
- *Read Genesis 18—20. This lesson references chapters 7 and 8 in* Be Obedient. *It will be helpful for you to have your Bible and a copy of the commentary available as you work through this lesson.*

## Getting Started

### From the Commentary

Abraham is given the title "Friend of God" in 2 Chronicles 20:7; Isaiah 41:8; and James 2:23; and he is the only person in the Bible to have it. Jesus called Lazarus His friend (John 11:11), and He calls "friends" all who believe on Him and obey Him (15:13–15). As His friends, we can share His love and fellowship, and we can know His will. "If we are beset by an unseen foe," wrote Vance Havner, "we are also befriended by an Unseen Friend. Great is our adversary but greater is our Ally."

Friendship involves ministry.

—*Be Obedient*, pages 93–94

1. What are the different ways Abraham was a friend to God as described in Genesis 18? What does it mean to be a friend to God? What are ways believers today can be friends to God?

*More to Consider: All ministry must first be to the Lord, for if we fail to be a blessing to the Lord, we will never be a blessing to others. How is this statement true of the Jewish priests (Ex. 28:1–4, 41; 29:1) and of God's servants in the early church (Acts 13:1–2)? (See also Col. 3:23–24.)*

2. Choose one verse or phrase from Genesis 18—20 that stands out to you. This could be something you're intrigued by, something that makes you uncomfortable, something that puzzles you, something that resonates with you, or just something you want to examine further. Write that here.

## Going Deeper

*From the Commentary*

> Because Abraham was faithful to the Lord, he became a channel of blessing to his wife and eventually to his family (Gen. 18:19). Sarah had an important role to play in the working out of God's plan of salvation for the world, and she did her part (Heb. 11:11; 1 Peter 3:1–7; Rom. 4:18–21). Sarah was now eighty-nine years old, yet she was still a desirable woman with charm and beauty (Gen. 20), partly because her husband loved her and treated her like the princess that she was.
>
> The Lord had come all the way from heaven to give Abraham and Sarah an announcement: At that same time next year, Sarah would give birth to the promised son! The news was so incredible that Sarah laughed and questioned whether such a thing could happen to two elderly people. Abraham's laughter had been born out of joyful faith (17:17), but Sarah's laughter was marked by unbelief, even though she tried to deny it.
>
> —*Be Obedient*, page 96

3. Review Genesis 18:9–15. How was Sarah's laughter marked by unbelief? How does doubting God play out in the way we live our lives? What are the practical results of doubting God? How does Romans 4:20–21 answer the question of doubt?

*From the Commentary*

> Abraham belonged to that select company of God's people
> known as intercessors, individuals like Moses, Samuel,
> Elijah, Jeremiah, the apostles, and our Lord Himself. In
> fact, our Lord's ministry today in heaven is a ministry of
> intercession (Rom. 8:34); so we are never more like our
> Lord than when we are interceding for others. It is not
> enough for us to be a blessing to our Lord and our home;
> we must also seek to win a lost world and bring sinners
> to the Savior.
>
> *—Be Obedient*, page 97

4. Why did the Lord linger while the angels went on to Sodom? (See Gen.
18:22—19:1.) How do Abraham's actions change from the first half of
Genesis 18 to the second half? What does this teach us about balance?

*From the Commentary*

> The cities of Sodom and Gomorrah were exceedingly
> wicked (Gen. 13:13) because the men of these cities were

given over to sexual practices that were contrary to nature (19:5; Jude 7; Rom. 1:27). The words *sodomy* and *sodomize* are synonyms for these homosexual practices. The men did not try to hide their sin (Isa. 3:9), nor would they repent (Jer. 23:14).

But why would Abraham want God to spare such wicked people? Far better that they should be wiped off the face of the earth! Of course, Abraham's first concern was for Lot and his family. In fact, Abraham had already rescued the people of Sodom solely because of Lot (Gen. 14:12–16), though none of the citizens seemed to appreciate what he had done for them. They all went right back into the old way of life and did not heed the warning of God.

—*Be Obedient*, page 98

5. How was the sudden destruction of Sodom and Gomorrah used in Scripture as an example of God's righteous judgment? (See Isa. 1:9; 3:9; Lam. 4:6; Zeph. 2:9; 2 Peter 2:6.) How did Jesus refer to the event? (See Luke 17:28–32.) Why did Abraham want to save the people? (See 2 Peter 3:9; 1 Tim. 2:4.)

## From the Commentary

> Genesis 19 records the sad consequences of Lot's spiritual decline; then Lot passes off the scene while Abraham's story continues (1 John 2:17). Abraham was the friend of God, but Lot was the friend of the world (James 4:4), and the contrasts between these two men are easy to see.
>
> Locations (Gen. 19:1).
>
> Times (Gen. 19:1).
>
> Visitors (Gen. 19:1).
>
> Hospitality (Gen. 19:2–11).
>
> Messages (Gen. 19:2–13).
>
> Influence (Gen. 19:14).
>
> Attitudes (Gen. 19:15–26).
>
> Consequences (Gen. 19:27–38).
>
> —*Be Obedient*, pages 99–101

6. Review each of the categories in the previous commentary excerpt (and the associated references in Genesis 19) as they contrast Abraham and Lot. What do these reveal about being a friend of the world? What does it mean to be a friend of the world today?

## From the Commentary

While it is true that the destruction of Sodom and Gomorrah is an example of God's righteous judgment (Jude 7), it is also true that God's love for lost sinners is clearly seen in this story. Jesus certainly did not approve of the lifestyle of the men of Sodom, but He came to save sinners just like those in Sodom and Gomorrah (Matt. 9:9–17). When He ministered on earth, He was known as "a friend of tax collectors and sinners" (11:19 NASB)—*and He was!*

Consider our Lord's love for the people of the wicked cities of the plain. To begin with, He was longsuffering toward them as He beheld their sin (Gen. 18:20; 19:13). Just as Abel's blood cried out to God from the ground (4:10), so the sins of the people cried out from the wicked cities. God is longsuffering and holds back His judgment so that sinners will have time to repent (2 Peter 3:1–9).

—*Be Obedient*, page 102

7. What does it mean to be long-suffering? How was God long-suffering in the situation with Sodom? Why did He listen to Abraham's intercession? How is God's offer to Abraham an example of grace? How is it evidence of His sovereignty?

## From the Commentary

> We usually think of Abraham as a man who was always
> performing great exploits of faith, and we forget that his
> daily life was somewhat routine. He had to take care of a
> pregnant wife and a young son, and he needed to manage
> great flocks and herds and handle the business affairs of
> the camp. Abraham and his chief steward were respon-
> sible for settling the daily disputes and making important
> decisions.
>
> In addition, there were neighbors to deal with—like
> Abimelech, the king of Gerar. In Abraham's dealings with
> his neighbors, the patriarch is seen first as a troublemaker
> (Gen. 20) and then as a peacemaker (21:22–34). As we
> study these two experiences, we can learn how to relate
> positively to those who are outside the faith and be better
> witnesses to them.
>
> —*Be Obedient*, pages 107–8

8. What can we learn from Abraham about how to deal with people outside
the faith? Why is this important to understand? (See also Col. 4:5; 1 Thess.
4:12; 1 Tim. 3:7.) Why is it sometimes challenging to deal with people who
aren't believers? What are some ways it's easier to deal with nonbelievers
than believers?

*More to Consider: Genesis 20 would be an embarrassment to us except for one thing: The Bible tells the truth about all people, and that includes God's people. (See these other examples: Gen. 9:20–23; Num. 20:1–13; 2 Sam. 11; Matt. 26:69–75; Gal. 2:13.) What do these stories teach us about being people of faith? What do they teach us about pride? (See 1 Cor. 10:12.)*

## From the Commentary

After arriving in Gerar, Abraham began to walk by sight and not by faith, for he began to be afraid (Gen. 20:11). Fear of man and faith in God cannot dwell together in the same heart. "The fear of man brings a snare, but whoever trusts in the LORD shall be safe" (Prov. 29:25 NKJV). Abraham forgot that his God was "the Almighty God" (Gen. 17:1), who could do anything (18:14) and who had covenanted to bless Abraham and Sarah.

But the basic cause of Abraham's failure was the sad fact that he and Sarah *had failed to judge this sin when they had dealt with it in Egypt* (12:10–20). They had admitted their sin to Pharaoh and confessed it to God, but the fact that it surfaced again indicates that they did not judge the sin and forsake it (Prov. 28:13). In fact, the sin had grown worse, for now *Sarah shared in telling the lie* (Gen. 20:5). A home kept together by a lie is in bad shape indeed.

—*Be Obedient*, page 109

9. What is the difference between admitting sin and confronting it? (See Ps. 51:17.) What is the right response to our sin? (See Ezek. 6:9; 36:31.) How did Abraham fail in this? How do people fail in this today?

## From the Commentary

> What a testimony: "God is with you in all that you do" (Gen. 21:22 NKJV). Abraham did not permit one lapse of faith to cripple him; he got right with God and made a new beginning. James Strahan said, "Men are not to be judged by the presence or absence of faults, but by the *direction* of their lives" (*Hebrew Ideals,* 142).
>
> —*Be Obedient,* page 114

10. How did Abraham recover from his failure? What does this reveal about Abraham's faith? About God's love for His people? How does God respond when we put ourselves in a place of humility after failure? (See Ps. 1:1–3.)

## Looking Inward

Take a moment to reflect on all that you've explored thus far in this study of Genesis 18—20. Review your notes and answers and think about how each of these things matters in your life today.

> *Tips for Small Groups: To get the most out of this section, form pairs or trios and have group members take turns answering these questions. Be honest and as open as you can in this discussion, but most of all, be encouraging and supportive of others. Be sensitive to those who are going through particularly difficult times and don't press for people to speak if they're uncomfortable doing so.*

11. What are some of the ways you've doubted God? Have you ever laughed in God's face about something He seemed to be telling you? Why do you think you responded that way? What does it look like to actively trust God even when it seems impossible?

12. What are some ways you're still a friend of the world even if you're also a friend to God? How do you decide if an action or behavior is friendly to God or friendly to the world? How can you become more like Abraham than Lot? What are practical things you can do to move in this direction?

13. How well do you deal with people outside your faith? What are the greatest challenges you face when dealing with nonbelievers or with believers whose opinions clash with yours? What role does trusting God play in each of these situations?

## Going Forward

14. Think of one or two things that you have learned that you'd like to work on in the coming week. Remember that this is all about quality, not quantity. It's better to work on one specific area of life and do it well than to work on many and do poorly (or to be so overwhelmed that you simply don't try).

Do you need to work on being a better friend to God than to the world? Be specific. Go back through Genesis 18—20 and put a star next to the phrase or verse that is most encouraging to you. Consider memorizing this verse.

*Real-Life Application Ideas: Abraham learned how to live with and reach out to people who didn't believe what he did. Think about the people in your life who don't share your beliefs. How well do you relate to them? What lessons can you take from the way Abraham dealt with people who disagreed with his beliefs to help with your own? Come up with practical actions you can take to better deal with the everyday challenges of working among people who don't share your faith. Then put them into practice and invite God to use your interactions to bring Himself to those other people.*

## Seeking Help

15. Write a prayer below (or simply pray one in silence), inviting God to work on your mind and heart in those areas you've noted in the Going Forward section. Be honest about your desires and fears.

*Notes for Small Groups:*

- *Look for ways to put into practice the things you wrote in the Going Forward section. Talk with other group members about your ideas and commit to being accountable to one another.*

- *During the coming week, ask the Holy Spirit to continue to reveal truth to you from what you've read and studied.*

- *Before you start the next lesson, read Genesis 21. For more in-depth lesson preparation, read chapter 9, "'A Time to Weep, a Time to Laugh,'" in* Be Obedient.

# A Time to Weep
## (GENESIS 21)

*Before you begin ...*
- *Pray for the Holy Spirit to reveal truth and wisdom as you go through this lesson.*
- *Read Genesis 21. This lesson references chapter 9 in* Be Obedient. *It will be helpful for you to have your Bible and a copy of the commentary available as you work through this lesson.*

## Getting Started

### From the Commentary

"The Christian life is a land of hills and valleys," said Scottish preacher George Morrison, basing his words on Deuteronomy 11:11. Solomon expressed the same idea when he wrote in Ecclesiastes 3:4 that "[there is] a time to weep, and a time to laugh." Heaven is a place of unending joy; hell is a place of unending suffering. But while we are here on earth, we must expect both joy and sorrow, laughter and tears. You cannot have hills without valleys.

This is especially true of family life, for the same people who bring us joy can also bring us sorrow. Relationships can become strained and then change overnight, and we wonder what happened to a happy home. A Chinese proverb says, "Nobody's family can hang out the sign 'Nothing the matter here.'"

—*Be Obedient*, page 119

1. How did Isaac's arrival affect Abraham and Sarah's life in positive ways? In negative ways? What were their joys? Their sorrows? What does the way they responded to the hills and valleys teach us about how to live the Christian life?

2. Choose one verse or phrase from Genesis 21 that stands out to you. This could be something you're intrigued by, something that makes you uncomfortable, something that puzzles you, something that resonates with you, or just something you want to examine further. Write that here.

# Going Deeper

*From the Commentary*

> Sarah had borne the burden of childlessness for many years, a heavy burden indeed in that culture and at that time. People must have smiled when they heard that her husband's name was Abraham, "father of a multitude." He was the father of *one* son, Ishmael, but that was far from a multitude, and Sarah had *never* given birth. But now all of her reproach was ended, and they were rejoicing in the arrival of their son.
>
> But the birth of Isaac involved much more than parental joy, for his birth meant the *fulfillment of God's promise.* When God had called Abraham, He promised to make of him a great nation that would bless the whole world (Gen. 12:1–3). Then He repeatedly promised to give the land of Canaan to Abraham's descendants (17:7) and to multiply them greatly (13:15–17). Abraham would be the father of the promised seed (15:4), and Sarah (not Hagar) would be the mother (17:19; 18:9–15).
>
> —*Be Obedient*, page 120

3. Review Genesis 21:1–7. What does the birth of Isaac reveal about God? Why was it important for Abraham and Sarah to believe God? What was the result of that belief? (See Heb. 11:8–13.)

*More to Consider: What did Isaac's birth reveal about the reward of patience? (See Heb. 6:12; 10:36.) What are other biblical examples of that reward? What are examples from Christian history?*

## From the Commentary

The birth of Isaac was certainly the revelation of God's power. That was one reason why God waited so long: He wanted Abraham and Sarah to be "as good as dead" so that their son's birth would be a miracle of God and not a marvel of human nature (Rom. 4:17–21). Abraham and Sarah experienced God's resurrection power in their lives because they yielded to Him and believed His Word. Faith in God's promises releases God's power (Eph. 3:20–21; Phil. 3:10), "for no word from God shall be void of power" (Luke 1:37 ASV).

—*Be Obedient*, pages 120–21

4. In what ways was Isaac's birth a step forward in accomplishing God's purpose? How is Isaac's birth similar to the birth of Jesus? Why does God seem to put the weight of His plan in the lives of tiny babies? (See also Ex. 1—2.)

## From Today's World

In the past, waiting wasn't an option—it was the only choice. But with the coming of the industrial revolution, then the Internet age, waiting became a thing of the past. Today, information is available at the click of a button. No longer do people have to wait in line to buy things—they can order them online and have them delivered right to their doorsteps. The phrase "good things come to those that wait" rarely comes up in a society built on speed of information and no-wait commerce.

5. What are the advantages of a world that moves as fast as ours does today over the days gone by when everything required waiting? What are the disadvantages? How does a society of "now" influence people's relationships with a Creator who still moves according to His own timetable? Is it harder or easier to wait on God in today's society than it was in Abraham's? Explain.

## From the Commentary

In Galatians 4:28–29, Paul makes it clear that Ishmael represents the believer's first birth (the flesh) and Isaac represents the second birth (the Spirit). Ishmael was "born of the flesh" because Abraham had not yet "died" and was still able to beget a son (Gen. 16). Isaac was "born of the Spirit" because by that time his parents were both "dead" and only God's power could have brought conception and birth. Ishmael was born first, because the natural comes before the spiritual (1 Cor. 15:46).

When you trust Jesus Christ, you experience a miracle birth from God (John 1:11–13), and it is the work of the Holy Spirit of God (John 3:1–8).

—*Be Obedient*, page 121

6. Review Genesis 21:8–13. In what ways did Abraham represent faith? How did Sarah represent grace? (See Gal. 4:24–28.) What did their actions reveal about Isaac's birth? (See Eph. 2:8–9.) How is Isaac's birth a picture of the way sinners enter the family of God? (See John 3:16–18.)

## From the Commentary

It is worth noting that, in the biblical record, God often rejected the firstborn and accepted the second-born. He rejected Cain and chose Abel (Gen. 4:1–15). He rejected Ishmael, Abraham's firstborn, and chose Isaac. He bypassed Esau, Isaac's firstborn, and chose Jacob (Rom. 9:8–13), and He chose Ephraim instead of Manasseh (Gen. 48). In Egypt, the Lord condemned *all* the first-born (Ex. 11—12) and spared only those who were "twice-born" because they were protected by faith in the blood of the lamb.

—*Be Obedient,* page 122

7. Why do you think there is such a pattern of rejection of the firstborn in Scripture? Is there a greater faith message in this? If so, what do you think it is?

## From the Commentary

Like every child of God, *Isaac experienced persecution* (Gen. 21:9; Gal. 4:29). Ishmael was apparently an obedi-ent son *until Isaac entered the family,* and then the "flesh" began to oppose "the Spirit." It has well been said that the old nature knows no law but the new nature needs no law, and this is certainly illustrated in Abraham's two sons.

Jewish children were usually weaned at about age three, so Ishmael was probably seventeen years old at the time

(Gen. 16:16). What arrogance that a boy of seventeen should torment a little boy of only three! But God had said that Ishmael would become "a wild donkey of a man" (16:12 NIV), and the prediction came true. The flesh and the Spirit are in conflict with each other and always will be until we see the Lord (Gal. 5:16–26).

When, like Isaac, you are born of the Spirit, *you are born rich* (Gen. 21:10). Isaac was the heir of all that his father owned, and God's children are "heirs of God, and joint-heirs with Christ" (Rom. 8:17). Abraham cared for Ishmael while the boy was in the home, but "Abraham gave all that he had unto Isaac" (Gen. 25:5).

—*Be Obedient*, page 123

8. Why are older siblings so often jealous of the younger in Bible stories? What does this reveal about the nature of humankind? About the need for a savior?

*More to Consider: Isaac was born free, while Ishmael was the son of a slave (Gal. 4:22). Read about freedom in Galatians 4:31—5:1. What does Christian freedom mean? Why would this have been an important message to the early followers of God? Why is this important to believers today?*

## From the Commentary

When you consider the facts about Hagar, you will better understand the relationship between law and grace in the Christian life.

To begin with, *Hagar was Abraham's second wife.* She was added alongside Sarah. Likewise, the law was "added" alongside God's already existing promises and was temporary (Gal. 3:19, 24–25). God did not start with law; He started with grace. His relationship to Adam and Eve was based on grace, not law, even though He did test them by means of one simple restriction (Gen. 2:15–17). The redemption of Israel from Egypt was an act of God's grace, as was His provision, the sacrifices, and priesthood. Before Moses gave the law, Israel was already in a covenant relationship with God ("married to God") through His promises to the patriarchs (Ex. 19:1–8).

Second, *Hagar was a servant.* "Wherefore then serveth the law?" Paul asks in Galatians 3:19, and he gives the answer. The law was God's servant (a "schoolmaster" or "child tutor") to keep the infant nation of Israel under control and prepare them for the coming of the Redeemer

(3:24–25; 4:1–5). The law was given to reveal sin (Rom. 3:20) but not to redeem us from sin. Grace does not serve law; it is law that serves grace! The law reveals our need for grace, and grace saves us completely apart from the works of the law (vv. 20, 28).

A third fact is obvious: *Hagar was never supposed to bear a child.* The law cannot give what only Jesus Christ can give: life (Gal. 3:21), righteousness (2:21), the Holy Spirit (3:2), or an eternal inheritance (v. 18). All of these blessings come only "by grace [Sarah] … through faith [Abraham]" (Eph. 2:8–9).

This leads to a fourth fact: *Hagar gave birth to a slave.* If you decide to live under the law, then you become a child of Hagar, a slave, for the law produces bondage and not freedom. The first doctrinal battle the church had to fight was on this very issue, and it was decided that sinners are saved wholly by grace, apart from keeping the law of Moses (Acts 15:1–32).

—*Be Obedient*, pages 124–25

9. Why is it important to understand the relationship between law and grace? Why is legalism a form of slavery? Why do believers today still pursue legalism? What is God's answer to legalism? (See Gal. 4:1–11.)

## From the Commentary

In spite of the pictures in some Sunday school papers and Bible story books, Ishmael was a teenager and not a child when this event took place. The word translated "child" can refer to a fetus (Ex. 21:22), newborn children (1:17–18), young children (1 Kings 17:21–23), or even young adults (12:8–14; Dan. 1:4ff.). In this case, it refers to a boy at least fifteen years old.

Ishmael and Hagar got lost in the wilderness, their water ran out, and they gave up in despair. This experience was quite different from the time Hagar first met God in the wilderness (Gen. 16:7ff.). Sixteen years before, she had found a fountain of water, but now she saw no hope at all. Apparently Hagar had forgotten the promises God had made concerning her son, but Ishmael must have remembered them, for he called on the Lord for help. God heard the lad's cries and rescued them both for Abraham's sake.

So often in the trials of life we fail to see the divine provisions God has made for us, and we forget the promises He has made to us. We open our hands to receive what we think we need instead of asking Him to open our eyes to see what we already have.

—*Be Obedient*, page 127

10. Why is it so easy to miss God's provisions when we're in the wilderness? What promises did Hagar and Ishmael forget when they were in the

desert? What does it take to find the answer to most of our problems? (See John 6:1–13; 21:1–6.)

## Looking Inward

Take a moment to reflect on all that you've explored thus far in this study of Genesis 21. Review your notes and answers and think about how each of these things matters in your life today.

> *Tips for Small Groups: To get the most out of this section, form pairs or trios and have group members take turns answering these questions. Be honest and as open as you can in this discussion, but most of all, be encouraging and supportive of others. Be sensitive to those who are going through particularly difficult times and don't press for people to speak if they're uncomfortable doing so.*

11. What are some of the things you don't like to wait for? How does society today accommodate those desires? What are some areas in life where you need more patience? How can faith in God help you find that patience?

12. Have you ever experienced sibling rivalry? If you've been jealous of a sibling or close friend, what prompted that jealousy? How is your relationship with God affected by jealousy? How can you move beyond jealousy?

13. Do you tend to embrace legalism or grace more readily? Why? What are the dangers of becoming legalistic in your faith? How have you seen that played out in your life? In the lives of those you know and love? What does it mean to live a life of grace? How does that grace allow you to respond to those who tend toward legalism?

## Going Forward

14. Think of one or two things that you have learned that you'd like to work on in the coming week. Remember that this is all about quality, not quantity. It's better to work on one specific area of life and do it well than

to work on many and do poorly (or to be so overwhelmed that you simply don't try).

Do you need to put an end to jealousy? Be specific. Go back through Genesis 21 and put a star next to the phrase or verse that is most encouraging to you. Consider memorizing this verse.

*Real-Life Application Ideas: The "legalism versus grace" conversation has raged for centuries, and it continues to be a challenge in the church today. But it also can be a challenge in individuals' lives. Take a look at the ways you tend toward legalism. What are some things you do or some beliefs you have that make you a "slave" like Ishmael? Where do you most experience grace like Isaac? Look for ways to move from legalism to grace in your application of daily faith. Then do those things.*

## Seeking Help

15. Write a prayer below (or simply pray one in silence), inviting God to work on your mind and heart in those areas you've noted in the Going Forward section. Be honest about your desires and fears.

*Notes for Small Groups:*

- *Look for ways to put into practice the things you wrote in the Going Forward section. Talk with other group members about your ideas and commit to being accountable to one another.*

- *During the coming week, ask the Holy Spirit to continue to reveal truth to you from what you've read and studied.*

- *Before you start the next lesson, read Genesis 22; 24. For more in-depth lesson preparation, read chapters 10 and 11, "The Greatest Test of All" and "Here Comes the Bride!" in* Be Obedient.

# The Test
## (GENESIS 22; 24)

*Before you begin …*
- *Pray for the Holy Spirit to reveal truth and wisdom as you go through this lesson.*
- *Read Genesis 22; 24. This lesson references chapters 10 and 11 in* Be Obedient. *It will be helpful for you to have your Bible and a copy of the commentary available as you work through this lesson.*

## Getting Started

### From the Commentary

In the "school of faith" we must have occasional tests, or we will never know where we are spiritually. Abraham had his share of tests right from the beginning. First was the "family test," when he had to leave his loved ones and step out by faith to go to a new land (Gen. 11:27—12:5). This was followed by the "famine test," which Abraham failed because he doubted God and went down to Egypt for help (12:10—13:4).

Once back in the land, Abraham passed the "fellowship test" when he gave Lot first choice in using the pastureland (vv. 5–18). He also passed the "fight test" when he defeated the kings (14:1–16), and the "fortune test" when he said no to Sodom's wealth (vv. 17–24). But he failed the "fatherhood test" when Sarah got impatient with God and suggested that Abraham have a child by Hagar (Gen. 16). When the time came to send Ishmael away, Abraham passed the "farewell test," even though it broke his heart (21:14–21).

Not every difficult experience in life is necessarily a personal test from God. (Of course, any experience could become a test or a temptation, depending on how we deal with it. See James 1:12–16.) Sometimes our own disobedience causes the pain or disappointment, as when Abraham went to Egypt (Gen. 12:10ff.) and to Gerar (Gen. 20). Sometimes our hurts are simply a part of normal human life: As we grow older, friends and loved ones relocate or even die, life changes around us, and we must make painful adjustments.

—*Be Obedient*, pages 132–33

1. Review Genesis 22:1–2. What is the role of tests in the life of a believer? How does God use tests to move His plan for the world forward? How do God's people usually react to tests? How do believers today react?

*More to Consider: Read James 1:12–16 and 1 Corinthians 10:13. Considering Abraham's story and what you read in these passages, what is the difference between trials and temptations? Do all believers face both trials and temptations? Why or why not?*

2. Choose one verse or phrase from Genesis 22; 24 that stands out to you. This could be something you're intrigued by, something that makes you uncomfortable, something that puzzles you, something that resonates with you, or just something you want to examine further. Write that here.

## Going Deeper

*From the Commentary*

> When God sends a trial to us, our first response is usually, "*Why*, Lord?" and then, "Why *me?*" Right away, we want God to give us explanations. Of course, we know that God has reasons for sending tests—perhaps to purify our faith (1 Peter 1:6–9), or perfect our character (James 1:1–4), or even to protect us from sin (2 Cor. 12:7–10)—but we fail to see how these things apply to us. The fact that we ask our Father for explanations suggests that we may not know ourselves as we should or God as we should.

Abraham heard God's word and immediately obeyed it by faith. He knew that God's will never contradicts God's promise, so he held on to the promise "in Isaac shall thy seed be called" (Gen. 21:12). Abraham believed that even if God allowed him to slay his son, He could raise Isaac from the dead (Heb. 11:17–19). *Faith does not demand explanations; faith rests on promises.*

—*Be Obedient*, page 134

3. Why do you think Abraham was able to accept God's test without further explanation? What does this say about how Abraham's faith had grown? What previous experiences helped to grow that faith?

## From the Commentary

Two statements reveal the emphasis of this passage: "God will provide himself a lamb for a burnt offering" (Gen. 22:8); and Jehovah-jireh (22:14), which means, "The Lord will see to it," that is, "The Lord will provide." As he climbed Mount Moriah with his son, Abraham was confident that God would meet every need.

On what could Abraham depend? He certainly could not depend on his feelings, for there must have been terrible pain within as he contemplated slaying his son on the altar. He loved his son, but he also loved his God and wanted to obey Him.

Nor could Abraham depend on other people. Sarah was at home, and the two servants who accompanied him were back at the camp. We thank God for friends and family members who can help us carry our burdens, but there are some trials in life that we must face alone. *It is only then that we can see what our Father really can do for us!*

Abraham could depend on the promise and provision of the Lord. He had already experienced the resurrection power of God in his own body (Rom. 4:19–21), so he knew that God could raise Isaac from the dead if that was His plan. Apparently no resurrections had taken place before that time, so Abraham was exercising great faith in God.

—*Be Obedient*, page 135

4. Review Genesis 22:6–14. This is perhaps the greatest illustration of faith recorded in the Bible. Why was Abraham able to believe in God's provision? How might this story have played out differently if Abraham hadn't grown closer to God through previous trials? What does this chapter in biblical history teach us about God? About humans?

## From the Commentary

> In times of testing, it is easy to think only about *our* needs and *our* burdens; instead, we should be focusing on bringing glory to Jesus Christ. We find ourselves asking "*How* can I get out of this?" instead of "*What* can I get out of this that will honor the Lord?" We sometimes waste our sufferings by neglecting or ignoring opportunities to reveal Jesus Christ to others who are watching us go through the furnace.
>
> If ever two suffering people revealed Jesus Christ, it was Abraham and Isaac on Mount Moriah. *Their experience is a picture of the Father and the Son and the cross* and is one of the most beautiful types of Christ found anywhere in the Old Testament. Jesus said to the Jews, "Your father Abraham rejoiced to see my day: and he saw it, and was glad" (John 8:56).

—*Be Obedient*, pages 136–37

5. How is the story of Abraham offering up Isaac a type of Christ act? What other parallels can you draw between the Abraham and Isaac story and the New Testament story of Jesus Christ?

## From the Commentary

There is always an "afterward" to the tests of life (Heb. 12:11; 1 Peter 5:10), because God never wastes suffering. "But he knoweth the way that I take: when he hath [tested] me, I shall come forth as gold" (Job 23:10). Abraham received several blessings from God because of his obedient faith.

To begin with, he received *a new approval from God* (Gen. 22:12). Abraham had described this whole difficult experience as "worship" (v. 5) because to him, that is what it was. He obeyed God's will and sought to please God's heart, and God commended him. It is worth it to go through trials if, at the end, the Father can say to us, "Well done!"

He received back *a new son*. Isaac and Abraham had been at the altar together, and Isaac was now a "living sacrifice" (Rom. 12:1–2). God gave Isaac to Abraham, and Abraham gave Isaac back to God. *We must be careful that God's gifts do not take the place of the Giver.*

God gave Abraham *new assurances* (Gen. 22:16–18). He had heard these promises before, but now they took on fresh new meaning. Charles Spurgeon used to say that the promises of God never shine brighter than in the furnace of affliction. What two men did on a lonely altar would one day bring blessing to the whole world!

—*Be Obedient*, page 139

6. Review Genesis 22:15–24. What made it possible for Abraham to refer to this sacrificial event as worship (v. 5)? What does this say about Abraham's heart? About his faith? What were the new assurances Abraham was given after God provided a lamb? Did this event change Abraham's life? Explain.

## From the Commentary

It seems strange that the longest chapter in Genesis tells the story of how a man got his wife. While that is an important topic, and this is certainly a beautiful story, does it deserve that much space? Only thirty-one verses are devoted to the creation account in Genesis 1; sixty-seven verses are allowed to relate how Rebekah became Isaac's wife. Why?

For one thing, the chapter emphasizes separation. Abraham made it clear that his son was not to marry a Canaanite woman (Gen. 24:3). The law of Moses did not permit the Jewish men to marry heathen women (Deut. 7:1–11). Nor are believers today to marry unbelievers (2 Cor. 6:14–18; 1 Cor. 7:39–40). Genesis 24 is a great encouragement for those who want God's will in the selection of a mate.

—*Be Obedient*, page 143

7. What are some of the practices referenced in Genesis 24 that are no longer culturally relevant? What are the lessons we can apply today from this chapter about marriage? How do we invite God's will into the selection of a mate?

## From the Commentary

Abraham was now 140 years old (Gen. 21:5; 25:20) and would live another thirty-five years (v. 7). His great concern was that, before he died, he would find a wife for his son Isaac. Only then could God fulfill His covenant promises to bless Abraham with many descendants and give them Canaan for their inheritance (12:1–3; 13:14–17; 15:18; 21:12). In those days, the parents made the marriage arrangements. A man and woman got married and then learned to love each other (24:67). In much of the world today, the pattern is different.

We do not know who this "eldest servant" was. If it was Eliezer (15:2), then he must have been very old; the events recorded in Genesis 15 occurred more than fifty years earlier. Abraham made him swear to three things: (1) he would not select a wife for Isaac from among

the Canaanite women; (2) he would choose her from
Abraham's relatives; and (3) he would not take Isaac back
to Abraham's former home.

—*Be Obedient*, page 144

8. Review Genesis 24:1–9. Why would this task have been difficult for the
servant? How did Abraham encourage the servant? (See Gen. 24:7, 39–41.)
What does this story teach us about how our faith in God extends to and
affects the lives of those around us?

*More to Consider: Just as Abraham wanted a bride for his son, so God
the Father elected to provide a bride for His beloved Son. In what
ways is the bride the Father's love gift to His Son? (See John 3:16;
17:2, 6, 9, 11–12, 24.) Why is this important?*

## From the Commentary

Neither Abraham nor Isaac went to find the bride; the task
was given to an anonymous servant, who was completely

devoted to Abraham. His favorite name for Abraham was "my master," which he used nineteen times in this narrative. He lived and served only to please his master, and that is a good example for us to follow today.

The servant got his orders from his master and did not change them. When he made his vow of obedience, he meant it and kept it. Whether his mission succeeded or failed, the servant knew he would have to give an account to his master, and he wanted to be able to do so without embarrassment (Rom. 14:10–12; 1 John 2:28).

But how would he go about finding the right woman for his master's son? *The servant acted by faith in the God of Abraham and Isaac* (Gen. 24:12). He believed the promise of God and trusted the providence of God to direct him (v. 27). He took time to pray and to ask God for help, and he kept his eyes open to see what God might do. In fact, while he was praying, God was sending the answer (Isa. 65:24). The servant was not impulsive but waited on the Lord to see what He might do (Gen. 24:21). "Whoever believes will not act hastily" (Isa. 28:16 NKJV).

—*Be Obedient*, page 146

9. In what ways are we called to be obedient to our "masters" today? Who are our masters? The servant acted from faith in Abraham's God. We don't know if he too was a believer, but he trusted his master. How is this story of the servant's obedience applicable to believers today?

## From the Commentary

Rebekah's brother and mother were willing for her to become Isaac's wife, but they wanted her to wait at least ten days before leaving home. This was a natural request, since the parents would want to spend as much time as possible with her and perhaps even invite the neighbors to celebrate with them (Gen. 31:25–27). Of course, they were delighted with the wealth the servant gave them, which was probably the marriage dowry, and no doubt they wanted to hear more about Isaac and the home Rebekah would share with him.

Just as the servant would not delay in presenting his petition (24:33), so he would not delay in completing his mission. When the Lord is at work, that is the time to keep going! He asked that they let Rebekah make the choice, and her reply was, "I will go." This is the decision every sinner must make if he or she is to be "married to Christ" and share His home in heaven.

What motivated Rebekah to make the right decision? She heard the word about Isaac and believed it. She saw the proof of his greatness, generosity, and wealth and wanted to belong to him for the rest of her life. She had never seen Isaac (1 Peter 1:8), but what she had heard about him convinced her to go to Canaan with the servant.

Her parents and friends could have given Rebekah many arguments for waiting or even for saying no. "You have never seen the man!" "Maybe the servant is a fraud!" "It's nearly five hundred miles to where Isaac lives. That's a long trip!" "You may never see your family again!" But she was determined to make the long, difficult journey and become the wife of a man she knew only by hearsay.

—*Be Obedient*, pages 148–49

10. Review Genesis 24:50–60. In what ways is this passage encouragement to not delay in responding to God's call? Can unsaved people "lose" the opportunity to belong to God if they don't act quickly? Explain. (See Heb. 3:7–8, 15; 2 Cor. 6:2.)

## Looking Inward

Take a moment to reflect on all that you've explored thus far in this study of Genesis 22; 24. Review your notes and answers and think about how each of these things matters in your life today.

*Tips for Small Groups: To get the most out of this section, form pairs or trios and have group members take turns answering these questions. Be honest and as open as you can in this discussion, but most of all, be encouraging and supportive of others. Be sensitive to those who are going through particularly difficult times and don't press for people to speak if they're uncomfortable doing so.*

11. What are some ways you rest on promises instead of asking God for explanation of circumstances? What are some areas of life where you've learned to trust God when previously you had a hard time doing so? What accounted for that growth?

12. What is the greatest sacrifice you've had to make for God? What does it feel like to be asked to sacrifice something? How does that experience bring you closer to Christ? In what ways does it stretch your faith?

13. Have you ever made an important decision because you trusted in someone else's faith? How can your faith be encouragement for another? How can it give that person the strength to accomplish a difficult task or endure a challenging time?

## Going Forward

14. Think of one or two things that you have learned that you'd like to work on in the coming week. Remember that this is all about quality, not quantity. It's better to work on one specific area of life and do it well than to work on many and do poorly (or to be so overwhelmed that you simply don't try).

Do you want to learn how to become more sacrificial in your relationship with God? Be specific. Go back through Genesis 22; 24 and put a star next to the phrase or verse that is most encouraging to you. Consider memorizing this verse.

*Real-Life Application Ideas: What are the biggest unknowns in your life right now? Think about family and relationship circumstances, job-related issues, and spiritual goals. What role does trust play in each of these circumstances? How do you know the difference between trusting God and simply not doing anything at all? Think of practical ways to pursue God's will in each of your uncertain circumstances, then act on those ideas, leaving plenty of room for God to speak into your direction.*

## Seeking Help

15. Write a prayer below (or simply pray one in silence), inviting God to work on your mind and heart in those areas you've noted in the Going Forward section. Be honest about your desires and fears.

*Notes for Small Groups:*

- *Look for ways to put into practice the things you wrote in the Going Forward section. Talk with other group members about your ideas and commit to being accountable to one another.*
- *During the coming week, ask the Holy Spirit to continue to reveal truth to you from what you've read and studied.*
- *Before you start the next lesson, read Genesis 23; 25. For more in-depth lesson preparation, read chapter 12, "'A Time to Die,'" in* Be Obedient.

# A Time to Die
## (GENESIS 23; 25)

*Before you begin …*

- *Pray for the Holy Spirit to reveal truth and wisdom as you go through this lesson.*
- *Read Genesis 23; 25. This lesson references chapter 12 in* Be Obedient. *It will be helpful for you to have your Bible and a copy of the commentary available as you work through this lesson.*

## Getting Started

*From the Commentary*

King Solomon said, "A good name is better than precious ointment; and the day of death than the day of one's birth" (Eccl. 7:1). He did not say that death is better than birth, for, after all, we must be born before we can die.

Solomon's point was that *the name* given to you at birth is like fragrant ointment, *and you must keep it that way until you die.* When you received your name at birth, nobody knew what you would make out of it, but at death, that name is either fragrant or putrid. If it is fragrant at death, then people can rejoice, for after death, nothing can change it. So, for a person with a good name, the day of death is better than the day of birth.

The names of Abraham and Sarah were fragrant in life and in death and are still fragrant today. In Genesis 23 and 25, we meet Abraham and Sarah at the end of life's road, and we learn from them what it means to die in faith.

—*Be Obedient*, page 155

1. What does it mean to die in faith? How did Abraham and Sarah do this? What does this say about the strength of their faith in God? How is this an example of spiritual integrity?

2. Choose one verse or phrase from Genesis 23; 25 that stands out to you. This could be something you're intrigued by, something that makes you uncomfortable, something that puzzles you, something that resonates with you, or just something you want to examine further. Write that here.

# Going Deeper

## *From the Commentary*

> Sarah had been a good wife to Abraham and a good mother to Isaac. Yes, she had her faults, as we all do, but God called her a princess (Gen. 17:15) and listed her with the heroes and heroines of faith (Heb. 11:11). The apostle Peter named her as a good example for Christian wives to follow (1 Peter 3:1–6), and Paul used her to illustrate the grace of God in the life of the believer (Gal. 4:21–31).
>
> —*Be Obedient*, pages 155–56

3. Review Genesis 23. What earned Sarah the honor of being listed with the heroes and heroines of the faith in Hebrews 11? In what ways was she a model of a good wife? How did she exemplify grace? What does her life teach us about how we ought to live today?

*More to Consider: God made us with the ability to weep, and He*
*expects us to cry. Even Jesus wept (John 11:35). Grieving is one of*
*God's gifts to help heal broken hearts when people we love are taken*
*from us in death. What was Paul's message to the Thessalonians*
*about weeping? (See 1 Thess. 4:13–18.) How is the grief of a believer*
*different from that of an unbeliever?*

## From the Commentary

Sarah died in faith (Heb. 11:11, 13), so Abraham knew
that she was in the Lord's care. In the Old Testament,
very little was revealed about the afterlife, but God's
people knew that God would receive them when they
died (Ps. 73:24).

The late Vance Havner had a wife named Sarah. Shortly
after her untimely death, I was with Dr. Havner at the
Moody Bible Institute, and I shared my condolences with
him.

"I'm sorry to hear you lost your wife," I said to him when
we met in the dining room.

He smiled and replied, "Son, when you know where
something is, *you haven't lost it.*"

For the believer, to be "absent from the body" means to
be "present with the Lord" (Phil. 1:21–23; 2 Cor. 5:1–8
NKJV); so Christians do not approach death with fear.
"Blessed are the dead which die in the Lord ... that they

may rest from their labours; and their works do follow them" (Rev. 14:13).

The death of the wicked is vividly described in Job 18, and what a fearful picture it is! When the wicked die, it is like putting out a light (vv. 5–6), trapping an animal or a bird (vv. 7–10), catching a criminal (vv. 11–14), or uprooting a tree (vv. 15–21). What a difference it makes when you know Jesus Christ as your Savior and as "the resurrection and the life" (John 11:25–26; 2 Tim. 1:10).

—*Be Obedient*, pages 156–57

4. How was Sarah's death a comfort to Abraham? How is his response to her death a comfort to believers today? What comfort can we take from death when we know little about what's to come? How is the way in which we respond to the death of a loved one indicative of our relationship with God?

## From Today's World

The process of mourning has changed since the time of Abraham and Sarah. And while it varies dramatically from culture to culture, from religion to religion, it's not unusual in America for mourners to spend very little time dedicated to the act of honoring the dearly departed. While the pain of losing a loved one probably is no less severe than it was thousands of years ago, the time we allot to remembering that person is notably less. American culture in particular often encourages people to "just keep moving forward" as a way to get back into the regular routines of life, as if mourning is something to leave behind as quickly as possible.

5. What are the benefits of taking the necessary time to mourn the loss of a loved one? Why does American culture preach a "suck it up" mentality about loss and pain? What do we lose by rushing through the mourning process? What can we learn from Abraham's mourning of Sarah to help us better mourn today?

## From the Commentary

> We cannot mourn over our dead forever; there comes a time when we must accept what has happened, face life, and fulfill our obligations to both the living and the dead. Because he was not a citizen of the land (Heb. 11:13), Abraham had to request a place to bury his wife. The truth was that Abraham owned the whole land. God had

given it to him, but there was no way he could convince his neighbors of that.

Like Abraham, God's people today are "pilgrims and strangers" in this present world (1 Peter 1:1; 2:11). We live in "tents" (2 Cor. 5:1–8), which one day will be taken down when we move to glory. When Paul wrote "the time of my departure is at hand" (2 Tim. 4:6), he used a military word that meant "to take down a tent and move on."

—*Be Obedient*, page 157

6. Read Philippians 3:20–21 and 1 John 3:1–3. What do these passages teach us about life and death? How did Abraham follow the truth of these passages in his burying of Sarah? How can we know when it is the right time to move on from mourning?

*From the Commentary*

The key phrase in Genesis 23, used seven times, is "bury my [the, thy] dead." Even though Sarah was gone, Abraham showed respect for her body and wanted to give it a proper burial. This is the pattern for God's people throughout the Scriptures. Neither the Old Testament Jews nor the New Testament Christians cremated their dead. Rather, they washed the body, wrapped it in clean cloth with spices, and placed it in the ground or in a tomb. While there may be some situations when cremation is the better way to dispose of the body, for the most part, Christians prefer burial. This is the way our Lord's body was handled after His death (Matt. 27:57–61), and Paul seems to teach burial in 1 Corinthians 15:35–46.

Abraham gave Sarah's body a proper burial *in view of the promised resurrection.* When God saves us, He saves the whole person, not just "the soul." The body has a future, and burial bears witness to our faith in the return of Christ and the resurrection of the body.

—*Be Obedient*, page 159

7. Why did Abraham choose to bury Sarah in the land God had given him instead of their former home in Ur? What does this say about Abraham's relationship with God? What does his decision to bury her body and not cremate her say about his hope for the resurrection?

## From the Commentary

When you get to the end of Genesis, you find that Abraham's tomb is quite full. Sarah was buried there, and then Abraham, Isaac, Rebekah, and Leah (Gen. 49:29–31); and then Jacob joined them (50:13). Genesis ends with a full tomb, but the four gospels end with an *empty* tomb! Jesus has conquered death and taken away its sting (1 Cor. 15:55–58). Because of His victory, we need not fear death or the grave.

Abraham owned the whole land, but the only piece of property that was legally his was *a tomb*. If the Lord Jesus does not return to take us to heaven, *the only piece of property each of us will own in this world will be a plot in the cemetery!*

—*Be Obedient*, page 160

8. How does 1 Timothy 6:7 speak to the fact that all Abraham owned in death was the tomb where his family was buried? In what ways had Abraham invested in eternal things? How does investment in eternal things change the way we view death? (See Matt. 6:19–34.)

*More to Consider: Grieving the loss of a loved one is a universal experience. But the experiences of those who love God and those who don't are decidedly different. Read 1 Peter 1:3 and Titus 2:11–14. How do these verses speak to that difference?*

## From the Commentary

After a person dies, we read the obituary, and after the burial, we read the will. Let's do that with Abraham.

Abraham died "in a good old age" as the Lord had promised him (Gen. 15:15). He had walked with the Lord for a century (12:4) and had been "the Friend of God" (James 2:23). Old age is "good" if you have the blessing of the Lord on your life (Prov. 16:31). In spite of physical deterioration and weakness, you can enjoy His presence and do His will until the very end (2 Cor. 4:16—5:8).

Like Sarah before him, Abraham "died in faith." For one hundred years, he had been a stranger and a pilgrim on the earth, seeking a heavenly country, and now his desires were fulfilled (Heb. 11:13–16). His life had not been an easy one, but he had walked by faith a day at a time, and the Lord had brought him through. Whenever Abraham failed the Lord, he returned to Him and started over again, and the Lord gave him a new beginning.

He also died "full of years" (Gen. 25:8). This suggests more than a quantity of time; it suggests a quality of life. James Strahan translates it "satisfied with life" (*Hebrew*

*Ideals*, 197). Abraham, who was flourishing and fruitful to the very end, fulfilled the picture of old age given in Psalm 92:12–15. How few people really experience joy and satisfaction when they reach old age! When they look back, it is with regret; when they look ahead, it is with fear; and when they look around, it is with complaint.

An anonymous wit claimed that he would rather be "over the hill" than under it. But death is not a threat to the person who trusts Jesus Christ and lives by His Word. Old age can be a time of rich experience in the Lord and wonderful opportunities to share Him with the next generation (Ps. 48:13–14; 78:5–7).

—*Be Obedient*, page 161

9. How does someone die "full of years" in today's world? What can old age offer that youth can't to the life of a believer? How do believers prepare themselves to meet the Lord with confidence in the afterlife?

## From the Commentary

Abraham left his material wealth to his family and his spiritual wealth to the whole world, all who would believe on Jesus Christ.

When God renewed Abraham's natural strength for the begetting of Isaac, He did not take that strength away, and Abraham was able to marry again and have another family. However, he made a distinction between these six new sons and his son Isaac, for Isaac was God's choice to carry on the covenant line. Keturah's sons received gifts, but Isaac received the inheritance and the blessings of the covenant.

All who have trusted Jesus Christ "as Isaac was, are the children of promise" (Gal. 4:28). This means that we have a share in Abraham's will!

—*Be Obedient*, page 163

10. What legacy did Abraham leave us? (See Rom. 4:1–5; Heb. 11; Gal. 3.) What example did Abraham give us for how to live a faithful life? (See James 2:14–26.) In what ways can we learn from Abraham how to walk by faith?

## Looking Inward

Take a moment to reflect on all that you've explored thus far in this study of Genesis 23; 25. Review your notes and answers and think about how each of these things matters in your life today.

*Tips for Small Groups: To get the most out of this section, form pairs or trios and have group members take turns answering these questions. Be honest and as open as you can in this discussion, but most of all, be encouraging and supportive of others. Be sensitive to those who are going through particularly difficult times and don't press for people to speak if they're uncomfortable doing so.*

11. How have you dealt with the loss of a loved one? What does your grieving process look like? What's the difference between mourning the loss of a fellow believer and a nonbeliever? What role does trust play in both situations?

12. In what ways are you investing in eternal things? What are some of the ways you're investing in earthly riches? Why is it tempting to invest in earthly things? How can you move more toward being an aggressive investor in eternal things instead?

13. What spiritual wealth will you leave when you die? What are some of the ways you've enriched others' lives and faith? What kind of legacy will follow you? If you don't like the look of your legacy today, what will you do to change it?

## Going Forward

14. Think of one or two things that you have learned that you'd like to work on in the coming week. Remember that this is all about quality, not quantity. It's better to work on one specific area of life and do it well than to work on many and do poorly (or to be so overwhelmed that you simply don't try).

Do you want to be better at investing in eternal riches? Be specific. Go back through Genesis 23; 25 and put a star next to the phrase or verse that is most encouraging to you. Consider memorizing this verse.

*Real-Life Application Ideas: The spiritual legacy you leave behind is probably as important as or more important than any other legacy you will leave. Think about what that would look like if tomorrow were your last day. What have you shared with your family? Your friends? Your coworkers? Look for opportunities in the coming days to share what you believe with others, and always keep an eye out for ways to live out those truths in practical, meaningful ways. You can't build a legacy overnight, but you can start building one today.*

## Seeking Help

15. Write a prayer below (or simply pray one in silence), inviting God to work on your mind and heart in those areas you've noted in the Going Forward section. Be honest about your desires and fears.

*Notes for Small Groups:*

- *Look for ways to put into practice the things you wrote in the Going Forward section. Talk with other group members about your ideas and commit to being accountable to one another.*

- *During the coming week, ask the Holy Spirit to continue to reveal truth to you from what you've read and studied.*

# Summary and Review

*Notes for Small Groups: This session is a summary and review of this book. Because of that, it is shorter than the previous lessons. If you are using this in a small-group setting, consider combining this lesson with a time of fellowship or a shared meal.*

*Before you begin ...*
- *Pray for the Holy Spirit to reveal truth and wisdom as you go through this lesson.*
- *Briefly review the notes you made in the previous sessions. You will refer back to previous sections throughout this bonus lesson.*

## Looking Back

1. Over the past eight lessons, you've examined Genesis 12—25. What expectations did you bring to this study? In what ways were those expectations met?

2. What is the most significant personal discovery you've made from this study?

3. What surprised you most about Abraham and Sarah's story? What, if anything, troubled you?

## Progress Report

4. Take a few moments to review the Going Forward sections of the previous lessons. How would you rate your progress for each of the things you chose to work on? What adjustments, if any, do you need to make to continue on the path toward spiritual maturity?

5. In what ways have you grown closer to Christ during this study? Take a moment to celebrate those things. Then think of areas where you feel you still need to grow and note those here. Make plans to revisit this study in a few weeks to review your growing faith.

## Things to Pray About

6. Genesis 12—25 is about obedience. As you reflect on the way Abraham responded to God in good times and in testing times, consider how you might grow your own obedience to God.

7. The messages in Genesis 12—25 also include trust and leaving a legacy of faith. Spend time praying for these topics.

8. Whether you've been studying this in a small group or on your own, there are many other Christians working through the very same issues you discovered when examining Genesis 12—25. Take time to pray for them, that God would reveal truth, that the Holy Spirit would guide you, and that each person might grow in spiritual maturity according to God's will.

## A Blessing of Encouragement

Studying the Bible is one of the best ways to learn how to be more like Christ. Thanks for taking this step. In closing, let this blessing precede you and follow you into the next week while you continue to marinate in God's Word:

*May God light your path to greater understanding as you review the truths found in Genesis 12—25 and consider how they can help you grow closer to Christ.*